Transformations:

Stories to Tell in the Classroom

Transformations:

Stories to Tell in the Classroom

Phil McDermott

Winchester, UK
Washington, USA

First published by Liberalis Books, 2015
Liberalis Books is an imprint of John Hunt Publishing Ltd., Laurel House, Station Approach,
Alresford, Hants, SO24 9JH, UK
office1@jhpbooks.net
www.liberalisbooks.com

For distributor details and how to order please visit the 'Ordering' section on our website.

Text copyright: Phil McDermott 2014

ISBN: 978 1 78279 824 8
Library of Congress Control Number: 2014949213

A CIP catalogue record for this book is available from the British Library.

Design: Stuart Davies

Printed in the USA by Edwards Brothers Malloy

We operate a distinctive and ethical publishing philosophy in all
areas of our business, from our global network of authors to
production and worldwide distribution.

CONTENTS

Introduction

These six stories are to be read aloud. They are each accompanied by a commentary and a set of Oracy exercises. The commentary is there to inform discussion after the tale is told and will arm the teacher to nudge the thinking about the story into different areas. The 'questions' and exercises are a means for the children to 'process' the story and engage in a deeper understanding of the oral text.

We are all storytellers. For the last twenty years I have made storytelling my way of life. I am very fortunate. For two decades, every day in every term I have been telling stories to children. Over that time my 'bag of stories' has grown so that I am no longer sure just how many I have. I have become skilled in this trade and yet until now have not written any of them down; the advantage of Literacy over Oracy is the passing of information without physical contact, and although my training sessions and workshops have included many teachers, I want to pass these tales on to people I will never have the pleasure of meeting.

This book is called *Transformations* because the tales include shape shifters, human and animal. The stories travel eastwards from Scotland to England, then around the globe, visiting West Africa, Pakistan, China and Japan. These tales have also lived a long time.

These stories are a shade different from the stories read by children in the classroom or school library. I have not sat at a table to compose them; they have been transcribed from recordings of my oral telling. The countless occasions and audiences with whom I have shared them over many years have shaped them. From the time that I first encountered them, by being told the tales or having read them, until now, they have been changed and moulded by the circumstances of my work. So it is not I who have authored these written versions, but the groups of children who, by the subtle shifts in their positions on the carpet or by their gasps and giggles in the hall, have been key to defining the final presentation of these tales.

Oral storytelling is a shared occasion; it requires ears, eyes and imaginations, and demands the physical presence of a group. Reading is a beautiful but solitary experience, defined by self-determination; we have a choice of what to read, what to skip over and what time and space we will devote to it. In contrast a storytelling session, especially in schools, is the servant of time. Energy is devoted to its organisation and attendance. The audience rarely if ever has a choice in the matter. It is the gathering of unlike minds for an occasion. It is special. It is live.

When the storyteller takes the first breath the resemblance to reading vanishes. In the space of a minute the 'drop' occurs – the children stop watching the storyteller and start watching the images they are generating in their minds. The images each child creates are unique yet the children are still physically part of a group, influenced by the sway and reaction of the people around them. The laughter, concern, empathy and anxiety are safe and joyful because they are shared, and the feelings can then be accentuated because of the secure enveloping presence of the group.

The children become immersed in language, sometimes rich and unfamiliar language. They begin to learn meaning through context and make subtle connections between sounds and words. They experience sentence structure in action, not dead on a page, and they see oral grammar at work, producing deeper meaning. This is not an alien concept to them. There are no hieroglyphs to decode; there is no struggle to read or write words, no impediment to understanding. This feels natural.

We are not born with a reading or writing brain, but we are hot-wired for narrative. Oral storytelling should be the elemental basis of all teaching of reading and writing and must come before all efforts in other literacy learning.

With a modern curriculum, however, storytelling must plead its case; it must be rigorous in pushing progress in achievement. Even for the under-7s, reasons must be submitted for telling a story on the carpet; it seems that pleasure and delight are not enough. This anti-childhood stance is missing a great opportunity. How many phonics lessons, recovery sessions and one-to-one interventions can be dropped by telling children stories every day? How rich and secure can the bond between teacher and class become when a story is shared, and for magpie-teachers, how many links to topics and literacy units can be made to support other learning? Any curriculum, however, cannot be totally at fault; it is also the de-skilling and demotivation of adults in schools that is the prime factor in the decline of storytelling in the formal learning environment.

In general, it seems modern teachers do not feel inclined or inspired to tell stories. Many say that they feel self-conscious or exposed, an experience similar to that of the boy in the story of 'The Scottish Laird'. Yet we think nothing of giving the whole school a rocket in a 'telling off' assembly, or praising individuals for their good work during the week, all in front of hundreds of children. However, it is the quality of exposure as a storyteller that is different. To tell a story one must assume equality with the listener, so the role of the teacher subtly changes. It is a true sharing. The only immediate desirable outcome is collective joy. One must also accept that children are not natural critics; they do not care about the quality of the vocal delivery or the accuracy of the 'voices'. They will not be judging you. When they are settled and focused they will stop watching you and they will begin to 'see' the story. All they really want to know is what happens next.

The sure way to become a wonderful storyteller is to tell stories again and again. You will find your voice, you will develop your style, and you will open up an indispensable resource to develop your practice.

This book contains six stories to tell. They are written in the language of the live event. They are easy to tell and flow without a stumble. Worth noting is that, when written down, they tend to mirror children's 'free' writing. There are few rich portrayals, rarely any adverbs, setting description is thin and the list of connectives is short. This is everything we rail against when teaching writing; our classrooms are wallpapered with connectives and 'wow' words. That is because we teach a particular form of narrative writing: we teach writing novels. The heart of children's 'free' writing is the narrative momentum, what happens next. That is what they first fell in love with. This eager anticipation of the fate of a character or the development of a plot powering towards a logical and satisfactory conclusion is the engine of a told story. This energetic drive mirrors their desire to explore the future, to see what is over the next hill. It is life-practice without jeopardy, a caged canary put down in the dark places. When we train them to write to a standard, we must be very careful to keep including that element that they love, that joyous energy; otherwise their writing may be perfect, grammatically and structurally, but will have no connection with their hearts.

Please read a story to your class once a week. Make it an occasion: include a candle, some music or a call-and-response introduction. Make time for questions or comments at the end. Have a look at the suggested exercise at the end of the story and formulate the 'questions' for some follow-up work.

Throughout this book I want you 'To Think', 'To Do' and 'To See':

- To think – about the nature and power of stories
- To do – the telling of stories
- To see – your observations of children.

After these six stories, seek out other books in this series or check out my website: www.thestoryemporium.co.uk, which contains over 90 video stories, including the stories in this book. The website also contains an Oracy-to-writing handbook and 240 lesson plans for use in the classroom.

Let's start making storytelling a class language habit. You will find it very useful in your practice, but be aware: the main reason for telling stories is for pleasure and delight, yours as well as theirs.

The Power of Stories

Positive Outcomes

If you want your children to be intelligent, read them fairy tales.
If you want them to be even more intelligent, read them more
fairy tales.
Albert Einstein

Stories are the easiest and most powerful way to increase children's learning skills in speaking, reading, writing and creativity. These stories can be an effective educational tool benefiting all children from the reluctant reader and writer to the high achiever, and combined with the children's evolving powers of comprehension, analysis, discussion and imagination, play an instrumental role in developing their literacy skills.

These stories will:

- Challenge and expand children's imagination
- Increase their confidence and enthusiasm for independent reading and writing
- Increase confidence and ability in speaking and listening in all settings
- Increase understanding of the language and image-making involved in storytelling and writing
- Increase children's ability to use language to explore their own experiences and imaginary worlds
- Increase children's understanding of plot, character and story structure
- Increase their skills, understanding and use of grammar and punctuation
- Increase and enrich their vocabulary, pronunciation and word recognition

- Increase their confidence in public speaking
- Increase their confidence in their own creative skills
- Lead to their personal growth and development
- Bind groups and classes together
- Create a unique sharing experience
- Give a creative boost to learning across the school and in the home.

Storytelling has always been part of the human experience. Stories are universal, crossing boundaries of language, culture and age. Oral stories have always been with us as an enjoyable and entertaining way to teach children human history, traditions, culture, morality and other complex ideas. Our stories help define who we are. Our sense of identity is forged by the stories we tell ourselves, and they can also help build and preserve a group's sense of community.

The importance of stories in the overall development of young children is well documented. Children's ability to grasp the concept of narrative appears at a very young age, and stories provide a key means to understand the world around them as well as other people and themselves. Stories mirror human thought. Evidence from neurology and psychology leads to the conclusion that humans think in narrative structures. Concepts conveyed in story form – more than ideas explained with logic and analysis – imprint themselves naturally into human minds.

There is also strong evidence to suggest that young children who are read to and told stories from a young age have considerable advantages at school, not only in the development of literacy skills, but also in the development of social skills, such as empathy and being able to relate to others.

The more stories that children know at an early age, the more likely that they will be successful as lifelong learners. But stories are not just for children; they are a communal activity, and if teachers and parents tell stories to children the positive effect is magnified.

The Fact, Fiction and Five Senses Questions

When telling a story to children something wonderful happens. After between 60 and 90 seconds the children stop watching the storyteller and begin to see the story. Their own imaginations begin to create their own unique version of the story. If you mention a wood, the boy from Somalia sees a completely different wood to the girl from Vietnam or from Middlesborough. Everybody in the room sees a different wood. It all depends on their life experience and their cultural references. Throughout the story the children's imaginations have created unique versions of the characters and backgrounds and even different readings of the plot. By the end of the tale there have been not one but thirty different stories told.

'... and that is the end of the story.' There is now a cacophony of voices from the carpet. The children are now vocalising the story. They are retelling it. Sometimes describing their best bits or just commenting on the experience. There is not a lot of listening going on. Often two children face each other and speak simultaneously. But this is not about listening. This is about processing and exploring the images they have made. The story is still fresh and live for them. The story is still continuing. It remains in the room.

I encourage teachers to savour these moments and not intervene. They must stay quietly watching. These are precious moments where the images are still being processed. After about two minutes the teacher brings the children to a central focus. I say two minutes because a confident speaker or dominant classroom personality may impose his or her own visual images onto the group. The teacher's task is to keep intact each child's unique imaging vision.

Now begins the exploration of those images. I ask that teachers refrain from soliciting generalisations and opinions about the quality of the story (Did you enjoy that? Wasn't it great when …?). The task is to begin a communal retelling, an exploration of the differences in the images perceived by each individual. One way to achieve this is the five questions.

There are three sets of five questions each. Each set has a different function.

- The Fact Questions
- The Fiction Questions
- The Five Senses Questions

The Fact Questions

These questions are there to re-establish the narrative of the story. In doing this they also recall the image for each child. They must be very general and basic, of the 'Who?', 'What?', 'Where?' variety. No description.

So for example, for 'Little Red Riding Hood' the questions could be:

- Who sent the child into the wood with a basket of food?
- Who did the child meet in the wood?
- Why was the child bringing food into the wood?
- What did the wolf put on before jumping into bed?
- Where was Granny when Red Riding Hood knocked at her door?

These do not have to be in narrative order. With older children it might be challenging to skip back and forth through the story along the narrative line. These questions are to establish the facts of the story. The facts give it its basic structure.

The Fiction Questions

Now we come to the differences in each child's perception of the story. These answers do not come from the story that has been told; they come from what each child 'saw' when watching the story. The teacher should explain that each answer is truthful because it comes from the child's imagination.

For example:

- What kind of basket was it?
- What colour is the wolf?
- Did you see any other animals in the wood?
- Does the woodcutter live in the wood?
- How would you describe the nightdress that the wolf is wearing?

Do not gainsay any of the answers to promote reality. If the basket is a Morrisons shopping trolley, well, perhaps that is what the child saw. We must never assume that our children might know what a basket is. In many ways their world is very different to the one we experienced at that age. By the same token, if one child saw a dinosaur in the wood we have to take that at face value, perhaps acknowledging that their wood is certainly a very dangerous place in that child's imagining. The other children will have their own opinion on this matter. But again all the 'pictures' seen by a child are valid at this stage.

The Five Senses Questions

Now we communally build up the detail of the story entirely from the imaginations of the group:

- Choose one scene in the story to explore.
- Repeat the question after every answer until you can judge it right to go on to the next question.

For example: Granny's cottage: Open the door. Stand in the entrance. Look inside.

What do you see?

- The bed. Where? Over there. (Points left)
- The cupboard. Where? Over there. (Points right)
- There is a glass with teeth in. By the bed.
- There are shoes by the door etc.

What do you smell?

- Food cooking. What kind of food?
- Flowers. On the table.
- Soap. Cleaning liquid.
- Wet clothes from the wash.
- The wolf's fur etc.

What do you hear?

- Snoring.
- Clock ticking.
- Silence.
- The birds outside etc.

What can you feel?

- The doorframe is rough wood. Splinters.
- It's cold inside the cottage.
- The carpet is soft.
- Spiders' webs etc.

What do you taste?

- This depends on the particular scene that is chosen. However, many children smell with their tongues and it may be worth giving it a try to see what responses can be had!

Image making is an essential part of writing. Pencils must not be picked up until the imagination is thoroughly exercised. Image making subsists within children, and the promotion of the idea that every child will see a different image, and that all the images are valid, will lead to richer and more complex writing.

The Sacred Space

This is the space at the front of the class, and the people who enter the space are worthy of respect and free from harm.

The Sacred Space is so called because it is a special place. It is an area, perhaps at the front of the class, that is used by children retelling, showing or inventing their narrative. Whether sitting on the carpet or at their tables, all the other children in the class are focused on the space. When a child steps into the space they take up a strong position commanding the attention of all the watchers. With use, children understand that the Sacred Space is an area within which anything can happen.

Some classes define the space using a rope or chalk line. This gives it extra appeal by creating a boundary to cross into the special area. Questions can be asked of children who are in the space, but it is important that no one enters the space unless they have stories to tell or other work to show.

When in the space a child becomes aware of exposure. Acute physical awareness in most children begins with the onset of puberty; until then children tend to look outwards from themselves. This is very different with the voice. The voice is the delicate expression of personality, and when used in a public forum like the Sacred Space there is a danger that the child will see the voice as a traitor, to be kept under strict control in case it reveals secrets. A function of the space then is to persuade the child to trust the voice. In using the space slowly, carefully and frequently, the child becomes acquainted with the voice and becomes familiar with its features. It begins to give pleasure to the child. The child becomes aware of its impact on others. There is also the sense that the voice becomes a generator for personal development, a mirror that reflects progress back to the child. The frequent use of words in public enables the subsistence of logic and grammar in language and clarifies meaning. It gives the child power, the power of understanding and the power of affect.

The vivid stimulus of a told story that sets off the tumbling of images has to be followed by a cascade of words. The narrative and action is so 'hot' in the imagination that children need to speak it out to comprehend it. Using the voice is imperative. It follows then that if Mother Kehoe's adage of 'the best way to learn something is to teach it' is true, then the Sacred Space exists not just for the working of the oral story but is also available for all teaching and learning. Let the idea of the public voice in action seep into maths and science. Let the public presentation of all work be the plenary of every lesson.

The Scottish Laird

A Tale from Scotland

One of the most beautiful birds in the world is the golden eagle. Golden eagles live in Scotland. Now, if you were a golden eagle and you were there on top of a mountain seeing the vast country spread out like a quilt below you, maybe you might take it into your head to fly. Take off! Begin to soar around the hills and mountains. Then look down. If you look down you may see a valley. In Scotland it's called a glen. And in that valley, there might be a lake, and in Scotland that's called a loch. And in the middle of the loch is an island. In the middle of an island is a castle. A Scottish castle – tall, sharp and black.

Well, in that castle was a lord. In Scotland he is known as the Laird. Well, the Laird said: "Right, chamberlain, come here. I have a got a wee bit of an idea. Well, winter is coming in and it's going to be a harsh one. It's going to get very cold indeed and I don't want people to be lacking in any cheer, so we are going to have a party. Invite everybody in this glen to the party."

The chamberlain, booted and cloaked, crossed to the bank and rode through the glen, inviting everyone to the party.

From warm smoky huts they emerged in their best clothes and with great excitement. Laughing and greeting each other, the people reached the loch and, getting into the boats, they were rowed across to the island and entered the castle. And as soon as they went through the big oak doors, they were greeted with the smell of roast meat and vegetables. And there in front of them five fires crackling in five hearths down the centre of the hall made the whole building beautiful and warm. Behind them were minstrels in the gallery playing music and every table was groaning with food and soon every bench was full of people.

Away at the far end of the Great Hall there was the Laird

himself with his family on the platform. Well, people were eating and drinking and dancing and singing and haut boys were darting in and out filling up jugs and cups with refreshments. After the food was eaten the Laird stood up and he took his mug and banged it down on the table. The minstrels stopped playing; everybody looked at the Laird.

The Laird said, "Everybody, I want your ears and your eyes. We are going to have a wee competition now, and in every competition there are winners. It's a storytelling competition. Over here, do you see, here I have ten bags of white pearls. These pearls will go to the ten best storytellers. But over here I have something special. This is a bag of black pearls. And this will go to the best story. Okay! You have all got stories. Let's hear them. Who's first?"

A young woman put up her hand.

"Ah, Morag, I know you from last year," said the Laird. "Come up! Let's have your story."

Morag got up and she started to tell a story. Her voice was quiet, but filled the room. Everyone was silent and the story was so heartbreakingly beautiful that there was not a dry eye in the whole building. When she had done, she got a roar of applause.

The Laird beamed. "Hey, Morag! You win the first bag of white pearls. Now, who's next?"

A man put his hand up.

The Laird was delighted. "A man from England! A visitor! Well, friend, you are a stranger no more. Come up here! You are a guest in our house. Now then, let's hear your story."

The man began. "Yeah, all right, eh hey, everybody! Ehaha, this is my first time. Ooh, tough crowd, ha ha. Well, let me tell you this story about … oh, you are going to love it. You are going to love this. There was this man, yeah right, there was this man, right, there was this man, right, and he was walking down a road. No. No. I am wrong. I am wrong. It was not a man; it was a woman. That's right. Good grief, what am I like? There was this woman, right, and she was walking down the road, right. No, it weren't a woman. No, no, it were a man. I was right first time. And he wasn't walking; he was riding a horse … that's right, he was riding a horse."

Well, he went on and on and on and on. By the time his story came to an end, everybody had their chins in their hands wearing impatience behind their polite smiles.

The Laird said, "Thank you very much, eh. Sit down and no pearls for you. Anybody else got stories?"

Well, the evening went on and they had stories that were sorrowful and harrowing, that were funny, that were mysterious, and that were ghostly. Soon every single bag of white pearls had been won. Everyone had told. But the bag of black pearls still sat there.

The Laird said, "Is there anyone here who has not told a story?"

And there was. It was one of the servants, one of the haut boys. He was hiding behind a pillar. He didn't want to get up there. He didn't want to tell a story. He just didn't want anyone looking at him. But he was spotted by a ham-faced man. "My Laird, over here! There's a wee boy here who hasn't had a turn!"

"Bring him up, bring him up!" said the Laird, and the poor boy had to be dragged up to the platform. He stood there shaking, not lifting his eyes. He didn't want to do this! He just wanted to be somewhere else.

The Laird sat back in his chair and said, "Right, boy, what story are you going to tell us then?"

And the boy then said something that you should never say in Scotland. The boy said, "I don't know any stories."

The Laird stretched his eyes and the people gasped. "You what? You don't know any stories? Are you not human? YOU DON'T KNOW ANY STORIES!?"

People began to laugh and point at him, and the Laird got so angry he leapt up, grabbed the boy by the ear and dragged him down the whole hallway. The boy managed to twist around and he caught sight of all the people as he was dragged past them. They were standing and laughing and pointing and calling him names. At the end of the Hall they got to the big oak doors and the servants opened them, letting the cold in. The Laird then lifted the boy up by his ears and booted him into the night.

The boy landed on his knees on the cobbles. He got straight up and he started to walk. He was so angry and he was so upset that he didn't know how far he was walking. He didn't know any stories; why didn't anyone believe him? He didn't know any stories! He didn't know how far he was walking. He walked straight out of the castle. He walked under the high windows of the Great Hall. He heard them all inside still laughing, laughing at him. He walked straight to the edge of the loch.

He needed to sit down, to bury himself away, and he didn't know it but he had stepped onto a boat. There in his shame he sat down. And the jolt of him sitting down released the boat from its mooring and it began to drift into the middle of the loch. Not knowing he was adrift, the boy sobbed, "I don't know any stories." He put his hand into the water.

Now some say that the border between the seen and the unseen is thinnest in winter. That's when the trees are asleep, but dreaming, and the ground becomes iron hard to block the admission of those dreams from above. They say that when it first snows in any year the land is immersed in a pool of glamour. Now if a snowflake hits still, fresh water, magic takes place.

The boy's hand was in the water. He didn't notice the low heavy clouds, he didn't notice the snowfall, he didn't notice the snowflake hit the surface. "AAHHHH!" he screamed. It was as if a pulse of electricity had run through the loch. "Aww, my hand, my hand!"

But when the boy looked at his hand he didn't recognise it. His hands had dirty fingernails, had small burn marks from the cooking fire; but these hands were long and slender and pale and beautiful. "These are not my hands. These are not my hands." He then looked at his clothes. "This is not my jerkin. This is not my jerkin." He was usually wearing a leather jerkin that was full of grease stains, but he wasn't wearing it any more. When he looked down, he was wearing a dress, a green dress, a soft velvet green dress.

"What's happening to me? What's happening to me?"

He looked over the side of the boat; the moon had glimpsed him through a break in the clouds and for a brief moment had turned the black water into a mirror. He could see his reflection and it wasn't his face that looked back. It was a woman's face.

A young woman with long red hair that trailed into the loch.

"What's happening to me? What's happening?"

In a panic he stood, and as he stood up the boat crashed into the other side of the loch and he fell out onto the land. He got up, he tried to run. He picked up his legs, but he wasn't used to running in a dress and he tripped over and he fell in the mud. His hands caked in mud, his dress covered in mud; he didn't notice that someone was watching him. Someone in the tree line, watching him.

He got up and wailed, "What's the matter with me?" Then he heard the voice.

It was a young man who stepped forward. Taking off his hat, he said, "M'lady, you seem to be in some distress. Please come, come with me, and come to my cottage. Please."

The boy held out his hand. The young man took the hand and shepherded the boy to the cottage.

It was a small poor cottage, leaning and tumbledown. "Mind your head, m'lady, as you go in," said the young man. "I have a warm fire for you. My mother and I live in this cottage on our own. My name is Hamish. Please sit down. Mother, will you get the lady a little bit of porridge?"

The boy sat in front of the fire. He looked into the flames and he looked at the pictures in the fire and he thought, *What's happening to me?* As the mud dried on his dress, he ate a bit of porridge and he fell asleep there by the fire.

The next evening the mother had made up a bed for him and he slept in the bed.

The following morning he got up and he looked up and he saw that the old lady was reaching up, trying to get a jar from a top shelf. And so the lady in the green dress stood up and said, "Please, old lady, let me do that for you. I am a wee bit taller than you." As she took down the jar and gave it to the old lady, she noticed that her hands were full of dust from the shelf, so she got a cloth and she cleaned the whole shelf. She then began to notice that parts of the cottage could do with a good clean. Obviously the old lady was now too old to keep it up, so she decided to do it herself.

She put all the furniture outside and she cleaned and mopped the whole cottage. She moved the furniture back in and polished it with a little bit of beeswax.

Hamish came back and said, "Oh my goodness! The place is so clean. Thank you, m'lady!"

"Oh, don't thank me, Hamish. You saved me from the boat and you fed me and have given me a bed. I want to help you, Hamish. I want to repay your kindness to me."

Hamish replied, "Well, I could use some help in the fields if you don't mind, but your hands are not fit."

"Don't worry about my hands. Have you got a pair of trousers?"

Well, Hamish did have a spare pair and she put them on. She took off her dress and put on a blouse and went out and worked with Hamish in the field.

Hamish had one field, but with her help he was able to open two more fields, break the ground and put the seeds down. The harvest that year was more than enough to feed the three of them and they were able for the first time in Hamish's life to sell their produce for money.

Well, it was a year now since she stepped out of that boat. That morning as usual she washed her hair, put a comb through it and stepped outside. As she did so, she saw Hamish on one knee in his best gear with his hat off and a bunch of flowers.

Hamish looked at her and said, "M'lady, will you marry me?"

She looked at him and said, "I will."

Well, they got married and of course they celebrated by opening another field. They had earned so much by selling their crops they could hire workers. After three years, they began to rebuild the cottage to a big house of stone.

It was in that third year that she became pregnant. She gave birth in the spring. It was the worst pain she had ever felt, but it was an agony instantly forgotten. Her little son in her arms banished fear and concern.

Well, in the fourth year that they were together they opened some more fields and she gave birth again, a daughter this time, healthy and strong. The fifth year was a bad year because the dear old woman, Hamish's mother, she died. Three months later a third child was born, then died at birth. When she held that third child, cold in her arms, she felt that she would never see another day of happiness. All pain dwindles, but never disappears.

Time went on and Hamish became an important man in the nearby town, and indeed she became a magistrate well known for her fair judgements. She was on the town council and people used to come to her from miles around for her very good advice. Soon her eldest child, her firstborn, he got married and now she was a grandmother.

Thirty years after her marriage her beautiful red hair was shot through with fine strands of silver.

Angus, her youngest boy, was 18 and one afternoon he said, "Mother, I have got something to tell you. Will you come for a walk with me?"

"Of course I will."

As she walked with her son Angus by the side of the loch, he said, "Mother, I hope you don't mind, but I have got my eye on a girl. She is very nice and her name is Janet."

"Oh, I know Janet; she will be a lovely wife for you, Angus."

Angus was delighted. "Oh, thanks, Mother! And you know what we will do when we are wed? We will clean up this loch – look at all the rubbish around. There are old pieces of rope, rubble and trumpery. See that old boat over there? That's one thing to get rid of."

She said, "Stop! I know that boat. I know that boat."

Angus warned, "Mother, don't get on that boat. It's probably rotten."

She wasn't listening. Her memory had stirred. "But I know this boat. How do I know it?"

She sat in the boat. She didn't realise it but the boat began to drift into the loch. "I know this boat." She put her hands in the water. As she did so, a snowflake hit the surface. The sky turned black. She shrieked in fear. She looked at her hands. "Oh no, no! No! No!" They weren't a woman's hands. The fingers held no wedding ring. They were the hands of a boy, burnt in places, with dirty fingernails. She called out, "No! Angus, help me!" She looked back; she couldn't see her son. "Angus! Angus! What's happening to me? What's happening to me?" She looked down and she was not wearing a dress but a leather jerkin with grease stains.

The boat crunched into the bank of the island. She got off and she started to run, run towards the castle. She got to the entrance of the Great Hall and she banged on the doors.

The huge doors opened and he fell on his face into the Hall. Everyone at the party looked round.

"I thought I just kicked him out five minutes ago?" exclaimed the Laird. "What are you doing back in here?"

The boy got up and said, "This can't be happening. This can't be happening."

Then the Laird really felt sorry for the boy and took pity on him. "Bring him up, bring him up. I was a bit harsh to you."

The boy was brought and stood beside the Laird in front of the whole assembly.

The Laird gently asked him, "What happened to you?"

The boy looked at the Laird and told him all about it. About the boat, about the magic. About meeting Hamish, about falling in love. About the joys of having children and grandchildren. The heartache of losing a child, the pride she had of being on the council. The story was long but greeted with rapt attention.

The Laird listened; everybody listened in complete silence. When he finished the Laird said, "That's the best story I have ever heard. Here, boy, there you go. A bag of black pearls. You have told the best story tonight."

Well, at the end of that night the boy took the pearls and he walked out of the glen and he walked to the city and he made himself a rich man with those pearls. He ran a business, he got married and he had a family. He loved his wife and his children and was a well-respected man in the town.

Often, though, at night with his wife asleep at his side, and his children dreaming quietly in the next room, he stared at the ceiling and pondered. He was the luckiest man in the world because he had lived two lives. But he was also the unluckiest man in the world, because he had lived two lives.

And that is the end of the story.

Commentary
When Snow Hits Water

I really enjoy telling this story. For the first third of it the audience is intrigued as to where the narrative is leading and the challenge is to keep them around until the transformation. Here it is important to set the scene quickly and to deliver the audience to a front-row seat in a strange world, in this case the medieval

Scottish Highlands. The eagle's eye is a useful device to cover distance and then to focus in on the Laird's chamber. The evocation of place and time renders unnecessary a physical description of characters. A lord is a lord and a servant is a servant. When children write, we rightly encourage them to provide detailed descriptions of people, but surely this is merely to arm them with choice and to practise skill, so that they can in future make the artistic decision to confine description to a phrase or drop it altogether and get on with the story. Especially with a live telling, action must follow narrative very quickly and description has to be effective but spare, or else an audience loses focus and things begin to get thrown.

The invitations to the guests and the subsequent gathering around the lakeside to be ferried across to the castle bring us all out of the cold and into the warmth and wonder of the Great Hall. We are with those people as they are awed by the vivid stimulus of colour, smell and sound that greets them as they enter. They can put the winter aside for a while and be together in good companionship.

Of course the main event of the evening is the storytelling competition. The prizes of pearls are strange and wonderful and signify the high status of the event, but they also indicate an otherworldly dimension, a clue that the evening holds a frisson of glamour.

The competition begins well with Morag, a seasoned story-teller, setting the bar high for others.

Then we have the man from England. To the dismay of everyone, particularly the Laird, his story is badly delivered, confused and, although enthusiastically told, not treated with the care that Morag has shown. This is a stranger trying to fit in to the occasion and miscalculating. Being from south of the border is not the reason for his ineptitude. There is a nonsense peddled about the place that English storytelling is dead, killed by the invention of the light bulb and buried by the post-industrial splintering of society. My teenage working life was filled with English men telling yarns with a skill that would make a cat listen. English humour is rife with the funny story; indeed English oral traditional storytelling is currently enjoying an expanding and sustainable presence in cultural life. I only made him English because I could do the voice.

In post-Celtic societies there remain many stories about the danger of not being able to tell a good tale; they often paint the refusnik not just as shy, but genuinely stumped when it comes to filling the vocal space with riveting narrative. Some of these cautionary tales are quick lessons, often cruel or funny, but leave the reluctant teller with a story to tell. They suggest that what is most important is not storytelling skill or confidence, but decent material. This is key when coaching child storytellers.

This is exactly what the main protagonist is – a child story-teller. The first time we see this haut boy he is hiding; he knows very well the potential for humiliation. At this point children listening to the story tend to lean in; they recognise his reluctance because they know that standing out in a public forum is filled with jeopardy. There are very few opportunities for children in a modern curriculum to experience that exposure, that prickle of awareness that being 'public' brings. Yet the only way to become proficient is to stand up and do it, but slowly, regularly and in a safe and secure environment. This process takes time, more time than we are willing to invest in a target-driven learning culture. Yet it is surely the case that, even with the rapid technological and social changes taking place as we slumber while delivering a circumscribed teaching and learning method, the actual person in a live encounter will be the deciding factor in the innumerable exchanges that affect our world. Our duty to children must be to provide a Public Oracy environment that is valued and encouraged as the means for children to take their place in the twenty-first-century world. No one expects every child to be an orator, but using spoken language in a rich, varied and confident way will open out the personality, clarify the thinking and raise confidence. It is not a guarantee of happiness but a secure route to reach for it.

The experience for the boy is everything he dreaded. The laughing crowd, the pointing fingers, the leering contorted faces. What is unexpected is the physical violence. This shows the outrage of the Laird that the boy has failed to meet expectations of the home and hearth in Celtic society. But the tone of the story has changed, the friendly gathering has soured, and as the boy's knees hit the cobbles after being booted out of the door of the Great Hall, the cold of the night presages danger. Here, as he walks distraught into the darkness, not knowing or caring where his feet are taking him, we see what is often a defining experience of boyhood. Men fondly remember the risk taking, the curiosity, the adventures, the friendships. We bury deep the embarrassments that change to anger, the humiliations that lead to rage. It is these deep cloudy memories that make men wary, suspicious, unable to trust, solitary, fearful. The boy will not find a woman to comfort him or a man to assure him. He waits alone for time to repair his shame. Some say that boys are the problem in school, the street, society, but surely it is our treatment of them that is the real omission. The boy moves quickly, unaware of his surroundings but still keenly hearing the laughter from the Hall; the boat for him is somewhere to sit, to hide. Since his entry into the story, everything has been leading up to this, the launch into magic.

It has always delighted me that old stories are infused with theories of particle physics, string theory and quantum tunnelling centuries before Einstein. It shows us that ancient people weren't less intelligent than us, merely that they held different views of what they saw. There are many stories from the Irish myths and Scottish legends that postulate that different dimensions exist at the same time but not particularly in the same space, and can be accessed by a rip in the membrane of reality. Magic is not merely the ability to concoct potions and cast spells but a quality of divergent thinking generated to access knowledge. The desire to explain the universe has been the consistent aim of ancient story-makers and is a human impulse that will always be with us.

Snow hitting water is the clash of matter in two different states. The magic is the reaction created by that event. Of course everything in the narrative until now has been possible – the geography, the meteorology, the occasion, the competition, the characters. It is when that pulse of magic surges through the boy's body and begins his transformation that we understand that we are not dealing in reportage but in story. Story, particularly fairy story (a fairy story rarely contains fairies), is always very relaxed about the truth. It upends science and mirrors religious faith: if it cannot be proved to be impossible, then it is possible. In a live storytelling setting, this is essential because it is this blurring of what we know to be real that begins to set the listener's mind to wander; it opens the door to the storyteller's great friend – trance. Trance now begins to help the listener deal with the inconsistencies of time and space, and allows the story to move on without the audience stopping everything and calling for an inquiry.

As audience to this tale, adults tend very much to behave as primary and elementary school children: they accept the events without question. The children are already in trance and have been since they were golden eagles flying over the glen. They have no problem with complete and instant gender reassignment; it is merely another twist in the road that will bring them to the end. Adults have also been with the story from the start, more like outside observers, approving or disapproving but never interfering. When the transformation occurs, a dreaming quality has entered the story and I see adults literally close their eyes. They have been given permission to relax their attitude to truth. At first I expected either giggles or dismissive guffaws from these sets of audience, but from a teenage audience I expected a stronger reaction. Nobody tells teenagers stories, except other teenagers. They are deemed too grown-up for a good, formal, for-pleasure story. After all, they are here, in our schools, to achieve! So it is with great pleasure that I venture, too rarely, into their schools to tell to them. Their reaction to this tale is more quizzical than sceptical: they are curious about the technical changes; they question other aspects of personality differences as well as the physical changes. They are prepared to accept. Magic here is not as important as relationships.

The long time that the boy spends as a woman is filled with the mundane: babies, building and business. If we ever fantasise about living a different life in extraordinary circumstances, for example going back in time, we tend to always be wealthy, probably male and with superb means of physical protection. We become time tourists. We want to wander through Victorian London, see the fall of Rome or be great pals of the Ming emperor. We would not choose a poor cottage in the Scottish Highlands without running water or maternity provision. This story is not about tourism, so in that sense it is not a fantasy but an examination of a truth about life. It conflates that life to a few paragraphs and, for all its leaving out of detail, it concentrates on the points in life which are markers. It sets us up perhaps to examine our own lives so far, which we indeed see as episodic, and with that it connects the boy's experience to us and stimulates our empathy. Seen through that prism, the boy's life is not mundane but urgent and profound. It is a life like ours. Perhaps story is relaxed about the truth in order to reveal it.

After her change back into a boy, the story rushes towards the end, having settled over the many tellings into the three-act structure with a prologue and epilogue. It is explained that his whole life as a woman has taken five minutes. The questions from teenagers especially focus on this time discrepancy: has the Great Hall been frozen in time? Does it exist at all within the bounds of the 'woman's' story? Does the second story continue without her, and how do they explain her disappearance? For the original audiences, the story maker(s?) would not have been concerned with these questions. The other life has disappeared and what is now important is the storytelling competition. Traditional stories are often like this; they do not bother with tying up loose ends and making everything neat. That only happens when tales are written down, when they are 'literised'. In their original form characters vanish, sub-plots evaporate and tales seem to switch direction totally. This has to reflect the priorities of the original audiences. This is a story about not being able to tell a story. This is pre-Freud and therefore not concerned with psychological meaning. The boy couldn't tell a story, and now he can. There is an element of cruelty in this cold stark lesson. It is that cruelty that marks this out as an old story; its concerns are not liberal, democratic or modern. After all, why bother protesting when someone kicks a cat when just outside the door is famine, disease, chaos and a short brutish existence?

This story was told to me by the wonderful Irish storyteller Kate Corkery. Stories are often shared between storytellers, but it is always a courtesy to ask permission to tell them, and how much the tale has changed under my care since I first heard it, I do not know. But for me it has now assumed its most efficient shape. When you tell it (having of course read it to your class the first time) it will change again. You will change it. When you pass it on to another, that part of you will remain with it for audiences not yet born. Who says time travel can't happen?

The Story on Another Tongue
Exercise: 30-Second Retelling

Retelling a story can be quite difficult. The images that the child has created are what they will be telling, and yet those images are in constant struggle with the words the storyteller has used. You will often find that the child will be able to use distinct words, phrases, even whole passages lifted from the story. With other children the scenes are unique and created by them in the moment. All of these retellings are valuable, none of them inappropriate. Be aware that stories always change on different tongues and it is useful to point this out; after all, that uniqueness is the seed of any written story that emerges from the sessions.

Although you told 'The Scottish Laird' to the group of children, each child experienced it on their own. However, this stance has to change. The child has to make that move from the private to the public; so all of that adventure that took place in the mind now has to be delivered to open faces and expectant heads on the carpet. This transition can be unnerving, so it is important to keep that same sense of community that the original story formed and transfer that to the children's telling. That is why in this session it is important that as many children as possible take a turn, so it is necessary to have them all tell for 30 seconds each.

Thirty seconds does not seem like a long time, but if a teller lacks energy, focus or commitment, the 30 seconds can seem like an hour. If, however, the teller approaches the Sacred Space with brio and confidence those 30 seconds can seem like three.

Ask the class the three sets of Fact, Fiction and Five Senses questions.

- Ask the children to tell the story from the beginning to their partner.
- After a few minutes tell them to swap and the partner takes up the story from where the other left off.
- After a time bring the children to a focus and explain that they will be doing the same thing in the Sacred Space.

Tell them that you are aware that nobody got to the end and that doesn't matter. They have warmed up their tongue, lips, teeth and imaginations.

- If they have to tell a bit that they haven't practised, they will just have to make it up.
- Give the children a number for their turn.
- Explain that if a child is in the space telling their 30 seconds, the child after them has to be standing ready to go.
- Tell them that this is because the whole exercise has to have pace. There is nothing worse than waiting until the next child strolls up and nonchalantly enters the space. It loses focus and energy. They need to run in to keep the story alive.

'The Scottish Laird' is a challenge to tell. It has many scenes and multiple characters. There is also the matter of the gender change and the subtle shift from 'he' to 'she' and back again.

- There is no doubt that, the first time round, children will forget scenes and incidents, but tell them that it doesn't matter.
- There is no doubt that the story will reach the end before all of the class have told, so explain that when the story starts again those children that haven't had a turn will have to pick up the scenes that the first tellers dropped.

The Sacred Space

This is the space at the front of the class, and the people who enter the space are worthy of respect and free from harm.

- After everyone has told, it is important to have a general discussion about the success of the task.
- It would be useful to ask the children to judge whether, if

someone saw the session and didn't know the story, they would be able to retell it themselves.

Remind them that when they hear a story it is best to tell it while it is still warm because, like the smell of a school dinner in the hall, the images can disappear by the end of the day.

Quick Tips

- To get an idea of how I tackled this story check out the video story 'The Scottish Laird' on my website: www.thestoryemporium.co.uk.
- In general don't worry about accuracy with accents. A neutral accent for the dialogue works just as well here as in any story. I would encourage you to give it a try, however; as well as discovering more about the attributes of vowels and consonants by rolling them around the mouth, the listening tends to sharpen and interest in the sound of language increases.
- Be aware of the change in sex and pronoun. It should slide in unnoticed.
- You may get a lot of 'and then, and then, and then' during the retelling. It may be good to have some connectives displayed, but this is not a priority. Getting to the end with as much rich detail as possible is the aim.

Kate Crackernuts

A Tale from England

So! Once, there was a king! And the king had a daughter. And her name was Anne. And she was the most beautiful girl in the whole country. But, sadly, the king's wife, Anne's mother, died, and the king remarried. He married a new queen who also had a daughter. The new queen's daughter was called Kate.

Now, Anne and Kate, they were the same age and they got on famously. They became firm and loyal and affectionate friends and they played together and grew up together. But the new queen, she began to get very jealous of Anne. She knew that Anne was prettier than her daughter Kate and she knew that Anne would be the first to marry. If that happened Anne would become the queen and not Kate.

So, one night, wrapped in a cloak, she left the castle and went down to the hen-wife's hut. The hen-wife was a witch. She entered the hen-wife's smoky hovel and said, "Make Anne ugly."

The hen-wife, who could see at once the cruelty in the new queen's eyes, said, "No problem." She took a cauldron from the wall and filled it with water, then put it on the fire to bubble and boil. She then put into the cauldron a sheep's head, sheep's skin and sheep's bones. She collected all the dead things from the forest floor and dropped them into the water. And the cauldron boiled.

A week later she said to the queen, "Send Anne to me, but make sure she eats nothing before she comes."

The queen called to Anne, "Go to the hen-wife's house for me; she has something I need."

Anne went down the stairs. It was before breakfast but, as she passed the kitchen, she saw a crust of bread and she thought, *Well, I haven't had anything to eat so I'll grab this crust and eat it.* She munched it, then off she went. She went to the hen-wife's hut. She went inside, blinking in the darkness.

The hen-wife said, "Anne, come in, look in my cauldron!" She lifted the lid, Anne looked in, and the stench coming out of the boiling water was awful. But nothing happened.

The hen-wife put the lid down and said, "Tell the queen to lock the kitchen door next time."

The queen was furious. She made sure the kitchen door was locked and said, "Anne, go again to the hen-wife, but don't have your breakfast; have your breakfast when you come back."

Anne went down the stairs, past the locked kitchen and into the garden, and there she met the gardener, and being a friendly girl, she got into conversation with the gardener. He was so pleased to be speaking to the princess that he offered her some peas that he'd gathered. She took three peas, ate them and went to the hen-wife's house. She opened the door, went in and the hen-wife said, "Anne, look in the cauldron."

Anne looked in – and nothing happened. But the stench was worse than yesterday.

"Make sure you tell the queen," said the hen-wife, "that you mustn't pass through the garden."

Well, the queen was even more furious and she decided to take Anne to the hen-wife herself. So, she grabbed Anne's hand the next day and she held it tight and dragged Anne to the hen-wife's hut and said, "Get inside, Anne."

The hen-wife said, "Anne, look in the cauldron."

Anne, with her empty stomach, looked in the cauldron and her head began to shrivel and her head began to wrinkle and her head began to fold in on itself and, all of a sudden, her head popped off and splashed into the cauldron. And the sheep's head shot up from the boiling water and stuck on Anne's shoulders.

"*Bah, bah, bah,*" bleated Anne, just like a terrified sheep, and she screamed and ran out. She ran straight to Kate and she tried to tell Kate what'd happened and Kate understood her.

Kate went to her mother and said, "That was an evil thing to do. Well, I don't want anything more to do with you."

She took Anne and she covered her big sheep's head with a shawl and they both escaped and fled into the countryside to seek their fortunes.

Well, they wandered far and wide by the lanes and the byways, begging for food. But what kept them alive was, every now and then, Kate would collect nuts and crack them in her apron and feed Anne and feed herself. She always had nuts.

Soon, they came to a castle. It was the castle of the neighbouring king. They went inside and they begged for work in the kitchens. That was a place where no one would question why Anne always kept her head covered. They worked very hard in the kitchens until, one day, they heard the rumour.

The rumour was that the king had two sons and one of them, the eldest, was very ill.

"What kind of illness?" said Kate.

"Well," said the cook, "it seems that he goes to bed at night but when he wakes up in the morning he's exhausted. He won't say nothing to nobody. He eats well but he's getting sicker and sicker and the king fears he will soon die."

Kate thought, *I think I can help the prince.* She went to the king and she said, "Let me have a try. I have a feeling in my bones that I can help him."

The king said, "You are among many that have tried, young kitchen maid, but since I am desperate I'll give you a chance."

So, that night, she crept up to the prince's room, but she didn't sit by the prince's bed like the other doctors and healers; she hid in the cupboard. The prince came in. The prince undressed, got into his pyjamas, got into bed. And Kate, in the cupboard, waited and waited and … then, at midnight, the prince sat bolt upright in his bed. He got up. He got dressed in his best clothes and went out of the room. Kate opened the cupboard and followed him.

The prince went downstairs. He went to the stables. He

saddled his horse. He called his dog, he mounted his horse and he started to gallop away, but Kate ran after him and jumped onto the horse and held on to the prince tight and they galloped through the night. They galloped through woods and, whenever she could, Kate gathered nuts, because she didn't know how long she'd be, and put them in her apron.

At last, the prince arrived outside a big, green hill and he said, "Open, open, open, green hill! Let through the prince, his horse and his hound." And Kate said quietly, "And the lady behind him." Well, the green hill opened and there was a tunnel. The prince galloped down the long tunnel with Kate hanging on behind him. After half an hour of riding, the prince stopped. He dismounted and, with his hound, he walked into a vast chamber.

Music filled the whole chamber and Kate followed him in, looked around, then hid in the shadows. And watched. And what she saw was this: lines of beautiful women dressed in ball gowns, all sitting along the sides of the chamber. They were waiting. But, as she looked closely, she saw that they were fairies – with their swept-back ears, their beautiful big amber eyes and their sharp elegant faces. And the scent of something wicked about them.

Well, the prince came to the middle of the hall and the first fairy, an exquisite one, stood up, approached the prince, and took the prince's hand. The music from the goblin band started to play and she began to swirl and dance with the prince, turning and spinning through the whole room. Kate watched, fascinated. The band stopped after an hour and the fairy, exhausted, handed the prince on to the next fairy who danced with him. No wonder the prince was so tired that he was wasting away!

But, in the shadows, Kate watched and she listened. And two of the fairies were talking and one said, "Sister, what news from outside?"

"The news is this," laughed the other fairy. "There is a girl working in the kitchens of the palace with the head of a sheep."

They laughed fit to burst.

Then the first said, "Do you see the baby over there playing with the wand? All that needs to be done is to tap that wand on the girl's head and she will get her own head back. They will never know that. They will never learn."

Well, Kate looked at the baby. The baby was playing with the wand. The baby with its baldy head and its yellow eyes and its pointed ears. Kate took some nuts out of her apron and rolled them to the baby. The baby looked at the nuts, forgot the wand altogether and started playing with the nuts. Kate grabbed the wand and put it in her apron.

At last, the prince had danced with all the fairies. It seemed like a whole week of nights had passed but, when they got on their horse and galloped home, only an hour had gone.

Well, the next morning, Kate got out of her cupboard, went downstairs, called her sister Anne and said, "Anne, be very still. Take off your veil."

"No, no," pleaded Anne.

"Please, take off your veil." Kate stared at the sheep's head with pity for her friend, then she tapped the sheep's head with the wand and, all of a sudden, it shrivelled and it wrinkled and it folded in on itself and it flew off and Anne's own head grew back.

"Sister Kate, thank you, thank you, thank you!"

Kate said, "Sister, my work is not yet done."

So, the next night, the same thing: she hid in the cupboard and, at midnight, the prince sat bolt upright, got changed into his dancing clothes, went down to the stables, saddled the horse and called his hound. Kate jumped up and grabbed the prince around the waist and they galloped through the night to the hill. And, once they got to the hill, the prince said, "Open, open, open, green hill! Let through the prince, his horse and his hound." Kate said quietly, "And his lady behind him." They galloped again down the tunnel. The poor prince once more had to dance with all the fairies while Kate waited in the shadows, near the baby, listening.

Two of the fairies, they talked to each other and one said, "What news from above, sister?"

"Oh, the news from above is that the prince is exhausted and will soon die and we'll have to get someone else to dance with us. If only they knew that the little flower that the baby is playing with is the source of this enchantment. If the prince eats the flower three times he will be cured of this dread disease of dancing. They will never know that. They will never learn."

Kate watched the baby play with the flower and she took some nuts and she rolled them to the baby. The baby forgot the flower and took the nuts. Kate reached out and carefully took the flower. When the prince had finally finished, she jumped up behind him on the horse, held on tight and they thundered back to the palace.

The next day the prince woke up. "Oh, I'm so tired, I can barely stand. I feel I'm dying." Kate came out of the cupboard. "Oh! What are you doing here?"

Kate said, "Peace now, my prince. I have something for you."

The prince looked at what she held. He reached for the flower. "It looks so delicious."

"It does. Let me break some off for you." She broke off the stem, gave it to the prince.

The prince ate the stem and he stood up out of bed. "I – I feel I can walk."

"Have some more." She broke off the petals and gave it to the prince.

The prince ate the petals and said, "I feel my heart is strong; I feel my blood is pumping."

And Kate said, "Eat the last."

And he ate the last of the flower, which was the middle, and said, "I feel better now than I have ever done. What is your name?"

"My name is Kate."

And the prince said, "I have a funny feeling, Kate. I feel you have been with me in a time of danger. I feel I'm falling in love with you." And Kate and the prince danced around the room, better than he'd ever danced with the fairies.

So, you can guess what happened. Kate married the handsome prince. And Anne, the beautiful girl who worked in the kitchens, well, everyone was amazed. She married the younger brother. And they all lived happily ever after.

And that is the end of the story.

Commentary
Kate the Good Friend

If Kate had suffered from an empathy deficiency or a nut allergy this story would have concluded with her as queen by the end of the first paragraph. For her the nuts are sustenance, a lucky charm and a means of distraction; they are Perseus' winged sandals, Theseus' ball of string and Baba Yaga's comb. The heart of this story, however, is friendship and sacrifice. Many fairy tales have stepmothers, which, given the period in which they were made, would be very common in families suffering high mortality rates and deaths in childbirth. In stories, most heads of families become kings and every queen is a means of carrying on his lineage. It follows then that stepchildren would be in competition to carry on the family line.

Many fairy tales have a good stepsister and a bad one ('Cinderella', 'Mother Holle'). Unusually, in this tale Kate, being the less favoured, is the heroine and acts against her own interest. For her the friendship she has developed with Anne has a far higher value than future security. Through their escape and sanctuary Kate is always there to help and protect Anne, and it is this capacity for care and compassion that helps the sickening prince. Not swords or spells but simple sympathy and keen curiosity are all the tools she has to defeat the bad magic. In older societies these two attributes were seen as the duty and the downfall of all women.

The fairy element of the story is fascinating. First the fairy hill, a common sight in a European landscape littered with the burial mounds and the covered-up remains of ancient settlements. Then the dancing. This sequence also appears in the Grimms' story 'The Twelve Dancing Princesses'. It is the compulsion to dance that suggests slavery to the whim of others. The fairies care nothing for their victim and abuse him for their own pleasure. They too have an addiction to dance, meeting every night in a large group until they have worn down the prince to death. They will then presumably seek another victim. The courtly ritual seems quite normal and almost banal. It is the aping of human society complete with ball gowns, the goblin band and the presence of the baby that makes the sequence horrific.

The under-the-hill scenes contrast with the inelegance of the hen-wife's magic. The sheep's head device is not subtle, but effective. The spell steals Anne's beauty and therefore her advantage. However, the story reveals that the real advantage is Kate's altruism and kindness, her sharp wits and resourcefulness, and her constancy in friendship. As such, this reads very much like a modern tale and Kate is an example that appeals to modern young women.

Freezing Kate
Exercise: Freeze-Frame Sequencing

The tale of 'Kate Crackernuts' has great energy and thunders along. The challenge, particularly with younger children, is to make sure they catch up with the tumbling of events. On a first reading many children will stay with a particular scene or image in their minds and dwell on it while the story continues; they will then refocus on the continuing events, having missed parts of the tale. When the children come to retelling the tale there is also the danger that they will miss out parts of the story through forgetfulness, or they may make a subconscious judgement that some scenes are irrelevant to the thrust of the narrative. In order to reuse the story as a teaching and learning stimulus, then, we must ensure that children sequence the events in the story accurately.

Because children 'see' the story in their imaginations, one sure way for them to order the story in sequence is by using 'freeze frames'. These snapshots of the story are made as interpretations of what they 'saw' as the story unfolded, so they contain within them those unique images.

Ask the class the three sets of Fact, Fiction and Five Senses questions.

- Ask the children in partners to choose a favourite 'bit' from the story. Tell them that it could be anything that they saw.
- Then ask the children to find a space, and with their partner freeze-frame that 'bit' in detail.
- Tell the children that a freeze frame is like a photograph and therefore is very detailed.
- Remind them that their freeze frame must be accurate because others will have to be able to guess what it is.

Observe the children and quietly prompt some of them to attempt more ambitious selections. Those who choose 'bits' that are not obvious (hiding in the cupboard, the goblin band, the death of the mother) are to be worthy of remark.

Sacred Space

When you feel that the children have completed their practice, ask them to sit down and face the Sacred Space.

This is the space at the front of the class, and the people who enter the space are worthy of respect and free from harm.

- Choose three partner groups and ask them to enter the space together and face the audience.
- Then ask those children to freeze their frames and hold the pose.
- Ask the audience to identify the frames in their partner groups without sharing their opinions with others.
- When you feel this has been done, choose one partner group from the audience to stand.
- Explain that the three freeze-frame groups in the Sacred Space are not necessarily in the correct narrative order.
- The partner group from the audience then steps into the Sacred Space and physically moves the freeze framers into the correct narrative order from left to right, as seen from the audience.
- When they have finished this, ask the audience if they have indeed moved the frames into the correct position.

At all times in this exercise you are encouraging debate and discussion among the children. Every time a child makes a choice or makes a case against another's choice, he or she brings the story back to mind and explores the technical detail of the tale. The Oracy they engage in enriches their language and promotes divergent thinking and this will have more impact on their development in Literacy than the closed questions of a comprehension exercise. It is also good fun.

- After the first three partners have been dismissed from their duties in the Sacred Space, continue with three more, as time allows.
- Repeating this freeze-frame and sequencing exercise will allow you to stand back and observe the children organising the session for themselves. The exercise can be used with any narrative stimulus.

Quick Tips

- To get an idea of how I tackled this story check out the video story 'Kate Crackernuts' on my website: www.thestoryemporium.co.uk.
- Be aware of the repeated passages in the story. They are what ancient audiences liked best!
- The detail in the freeze frames includes facial expressions, however difficult they are to hold!
- Record the session with photographs. It would be good for each partner group to draw their freeze frame.

I Know a Man

A Tale from West Africa

Long, long ago in Africa, in a country that now is called Nigeria, there was a king and he was a very FAT king. It is good to have a fat king because if you have a fat king there is a lot of food around, and this king was well beloved by his people because he liked to share everything he had.

But the king, although he was popular, was also very sad because his wife had died and he loved her dearly. But before she died, she gave birth to a daughter, a beautiful little girl, and she was the most beautiful little baby in Africa. She was loved and treasured by everyone in her village and when she was 18 the whole of Africa knew about her beauty. Well, she was so beautiful that many men wanted to marry her. Soon all the handsome men from all the surrounding villages came in to ask for her hand in marriage and when they came in, they walked like handsome men walk: tall, slow and easy.

They came up to the princess and, showing her their muscles, they said, "Hey, Princess, have a look at that!" Then stepping up onto rocks they said, "Oi, Princess, have a look at that leg!" Then grinning at her they said, "Oi, Princess, have a look at that face! What do you think? What do you think? Aren't I the greatest?"

The princess would say, "Yeah, I like your leg, I like your muscles and I like your face; it is just that – and this is the nasty bit – I don't like you!"

And all the handsome men, they slumped their shoulders and they shuffled out of the village not like handsome men at all, but like sad meerkats.

Well! This drove the king mad! You see, the king wanted his daughter to get married because there is one thing that a daddy really wants, and that's grandchildren.

You see, when you have grandchildren, you can call them and they will come waddling to you, their arms out. You can then grab them and you can throw them up in the air and catch them and then throw them up in the air and catch them and you don't have to change their nappies or feed them or anything. You just give them back to Mum and Dad when you've finished playing. So he used to say, "Please, daughter, get married! I want to have grandchildren!"

His daughter, though, would always reply, "No, Daddy! I am not going to get married because I haven't seen a man who is handsome enough yet."

Well, one day the princess and her friends were swimming, and they were swimming in the deepest lake in Africa. And they were talking: "Well, you know, I said to him, and then he said to me, and then I said to him, and then he said to me ..." But they hadn't noticed that they were being watched. They were not being watched from the banks of the lake, oh no. They were being watched from the bottom of the lake. Because there at the bottom of the lake, buried in the mud, was a PYTHON!

A python is an enormous snake that is about as thick as a storm drain. The python looked up and it could see the legs of the princess and her friends swimming and it wanted the princess. It didn't want to marry the princess; it wanted to eat the princess. And that night, when the girls went back to the village and the gates were locked, the python swam to the surface of the lake and then slithered onto the bank.

It then did something that pythons don't normally do. It stood up on its tail. Just below its head, shoulders began to form, and then arms and hands began to grow out of its shoulders. Its tail then split in two and legs formed, and out of the tips of the old tail, long toes grew. Then its jaw cracked and broke, and its eyes, that jutted out from the side of its head, began to move around to the front. It opened its mouth and all its snake's teeth fell out and human teeth grew instead. Its tongue first tasted the air, and then

46

fused together. The last change that the python made was that its skin transformed from mottled green to beautiful shiny black! Now he was a man, but not just any man. He was now the most handsome man that there has ever been, or will ever be, in the history of the world.

When all the changes had taken place, when the moon, hanging like a platinum disc, sank below the horizon and the day began, the snake, or rather the handsome man, began to stroll into the village.

As he strolled through the gates he passed some women who were crushing up manioc. They looked up and saw the handsome man. They couldn't help themselves. They stretched their eyes and dropped their jaws. One woman, who was wearing a red-patterned dress, shrieked. The handsome man looked at them, waved and said, "Hello, ladies! Nice dress!"

The red-dress woman fainted into the arms of the others. When she opened her eyes she said, "He spoke to me! He spoke to me." She then fainted again.

He continued to stroll through the village, making everyone stop and stare at how good-looking he was.

It happened that the princess saw him walking by from her window and she pointed at the handsome man and said, "Daddy! Daddy! I want that one there, I want that one there! That one there, I want that one there!"

So the king said with great excitement, "Chamberlain, go and get that handsome man! I think my daughter wants to marry him." The chamberlain hurried out.

But when the chamberlain came back he said, "My lord! That handsome man, there is something dodgy about him! There is something 'DOUBLE DODGY' about him. I think he is a wrong'un."

"What do you mean, chamberlain?" said the king. "Go away! You are going to spoil everything. My daughter wants to marry him. At last!"

The handsome man came into the hut. The handsome man bowed to the king and said, "My lord! Not only are you a very fat king – congratulations, by the way, on being so very portly ..."

"Thank you kindly," said the king.

"... you are also a very handsome king. Now I know where your daughter gets her beautiful looks from."

"Oh," said the king, "what good manners! You can marry my daughter."

Now in some countries before you get married, what you have to do is this. You have to hold hands with the person you are going to marry and walk in the jungle for a day and a night. Now if you find that you really still like that person when you come out of the jungle, you can marry them. But if you find out something that you do not like about them in the jungle, you don't have to marry them. It is a good system.

Well! The princess took the handsome man's hand and, waved off by the rest of the village, they started to walk into the jungle.

Later, as they were walking, the handsome man said, "My princess, look over there! See that bird of paradise? You are more beautiful than that bird of paradise."

"Oh! Thank you very much," she replied.

As they walked further the handsome man said, "Princess, see that lion over there?"

"Yes, I know. I'm feeling a bit scared." She took his arm.

"Don't worry. Last week I beat up that lion."

"Gosh, you are so brave and strong."

They walked deeper and deeper into the heart of the forest, until they got to a handkerchief tree and the handsome man said, "Princess, you just sit down here beside this tree. I just have to go behind that bush over there for, um, you know."

"Okay!" she smiled. "Don't be too long."

"I won't!"

But when the handsome man went behind the bush, the first thing that happened was that he opened his mouth and all his human teeth fell out, tinkling onto the ground, and snake teeth grew instead. Then his legs began to fuse together and his arms retracted into his body. His skull split and his eyes moved to the side of his scaly head; his tongue split in two and began to taste the air. The last thing to happen was his skin changed from beautiful, shiny black to mottled green.

Slowly the BIG PYTHON slithered from behind the bush along the forest floor towards the princess!

The princess, admiring her nails, said, "Are you finished yet?"

The snake didn't answer. It opened its jaws and swallowed the top half of the princess. The princess's legs were kicking, trying to get free. The snake gulped her down, slithered to the bank of the deepest lake in Africa and slipped beneath the surface of the water.

Well! The king was waiting at the village gate for his daughter. "Where are they? It has been two days. They should be back by now."

People said, "Oh, don't worry, sire. They are probably having a good time."

"What do you mean, 'Don't worry'? I am the daddy. Of course I am going to worry."

Three days later, the king was tearing his hair out. "Oh, chamberlain! What am I going to do? I want to go into the jungle to find them, but nobody in this village is good at tracking, or following a trail. We're all farmers. Oh, chamberlain, what am I going to do?"

The chamberlain pointed his finger to the sky and said, "I KNOW A MAN who is so good at tracking, he can follow the trail of a mosquito through the air."

The king said, "BRING THAT MAN TO ME!"

Well, that man came, the tracking man. The tracking man had a very, very long nose because he could sniff anything.

"Yeah! Yeah! Yeah! Here I am. Ready to do my job. I can smell anything, see. Oh! Oh my goodness, get that boy downwind of me. That is a very nasty boy. Now then, what do you want me to do?"

"I want you to find my daughter lost in the forest," ordered the king.

"Give me something that belongs to your daughter – oh yes, a handkerchief. That will do nicely." He closed his eyes and for a long while he sniffed the handkerchief.

"Follow me," said the long-nosed sniffing man. "I know where they went. Follow me!"

So the whole village followed him into the trees and through the jungle. After a few hours he stopped and said, "They both stopped here and then he pointed at some parrot, I think, or some other bird, and said something. Then they went on, this way!"

After another while he stopped again and said, "They stopped here, both of them. Then he looked over there at a leopard, I think, and he did a bit of boasting. After that they went this way."

They all followed him and went all the way to the middle of the jungle until they got to the handkerchief tree.

"Now, she sat down here but he didn't. No, no. He didn't. He moved this way; he went behind this bush. Oh dear! My lord, look at the ground. See all the human teeth. I am sorry to have to tell you that handsome man turned into a snake – a python, I think. I am not sure. Then he moved, slithered. See the marks? There was a bit of a struggle here. He ate the princess here. Then, look at his tracks. They lead down to the lake. He went into the water here, then he disappeared beneath the surface of the lake."

The king spoke with great sadness and anger. "No! My daughter. Swallowed by a python and now in its belly at the bottom of the lake. I want that python! I will rescue my daughter! But my people are no good at holding their breath; they can't go down to the bottom of the lake. That lake is the deepest in Africa. Oh, chamberlain! What am I going to do?"

The chamberlain pointed his finger to the sky and said, "I KNOW A MAN who is so thirsty that he can drink the lake dry."

The king said, "BRING THAT MAN TO ME!"

Well, the thirsty man came and he was really thirsty. He was so used to drinking water that he had a very fat belly, but because his belly was empty, he tied it in a knot and put it over his shoulder. He staggered into the village with his tongue hanging out. "The inside of my mouth is like a dusty desert. I will die if I don't drink. Somebody give me a drink! Please, please give me something to drink!"

The king made sure no one went near him. "Don't give him anything ... Come here, thirsty man, this way, this way ... Don't give him anything to drink!"

They led him to the deepest lake in Africa and the king said, "See that lake? Drink it dry!"

"Oh, thank you!" cried the thirsty man as he fell onto his front, plunged his head into the lake and started to drink: *"Glug! Glug! Glug!"*

Soon he had drunk the top of the lake and now couldn't reach the water. "Hang on to my legs!" he cried. The chamberlain grabbed his ankles and lowered him further into the water.

"Okay! Here we go. *Glug! Glug! Glug!* Hang on to his legs!" cried the thirsty man, and someone else grabbed the chamberlain's ankles and lowered them both into the lake.

By the time the lake had been drunk dry by the thirsty man, every villager was holding a pair of ankles, and someone else was holding their ankles, so that they made a chain of ankle holding from the bank to the bottom of the lake, with the thirsty man at the end.

All the water in the lake was now in the belly of the thirsty man, so he waddled away to find a toilet.

The villagers now lined the bank of the lake and looked down to the bottom. The bottom of the lake was covered by black, sucking, stinking slimy mud. Quicksand.

The king said, "I know that snake is under that mud but I can't send any of my people down there. They will get sucked down and disappear. Oh, chamberlain! What am I going to do?"

And the chamberlain pointed his finger to the sky and said, "I KNOW A MAN whose arms are so long that he can reach the bottom of the lake."

The king said, "BRING THAT MAN TO ME!"

Well, the long-armed man came to the village and his arms were over a mile long. As he walked, his arms dragged behind him in the dust. "Hey! Hey! Get those children off my hands. This isn't a funfair ride! Now, Your Majesty, what do you want me to do?"

The king said, "Throw your arms in there and find the snake at the bottom of the lake!"

"Okay! Out of the way, everybody!" ordered the long-armed man.

The villagers gave him room. He swung his long arms high in the air and they came down and landed in the mud at the bottom of the lake with a squelch. His hands then began to feel through the mud for the snake.

"Right, I am searching the mud! I am searching the mud! Oh! Found a spear."

"That's mine!" piped up one of the villagers.

"I'll get it for you later."

Everyone was very quiet on the banks of the lake. They were all watching the long-armed man moving his fingers through the slime. "I have found it!" he whispered. "I have found the tail of the snake. I will now slowly and carefully put my hands around the tail. Everybody in the village, hold on to me; then when I say, 'Pull', you all pull!" Everyone held on to the long-armed man, and each other, and braced themselves. "One! Two! Three! Pull!!!!!"

Everybody pulled with all their might. The snake came unstuck, shot out of the mud and whipped around, flicking black stinking slime everywhere. The villagers landed the snake on the banks, but it raised its ugly head, looked around, hissed – and everyone ran.

The snake slithered through the village, heading to the jungle, but the king was behind a hut and he had an axe. As soon as the snake appeared he chopped the snake's head off with a mighty blow. The villagers cheered. They rolled the snake onto its back. The king took a knife and opened up the snake's belly. When they pulled back the folds of skin they saw her. The princess. She lay in the snake's belly just as if she were sleeping. When the king put his hand on her cheek, however, it was cold, stone cold. The princess was dead.

The crowd bowed their heads and the king's heart broke. Through his tears the king said, "Chamberlain, all the work we did was for nothing. All the help that all those strangers gave us was in vain. My dear daughter is dead and there is nothing anybody can do."

Then the chamberlain pointed his finger to the sky and said, "I KNOW A MAN who can bring dead princesses back to life."

The king looked at him in astonishment and said, "BRING THAT MAN TO ME!"

The man came and he was a vibrating man. He quivered and trembled from the top of his head to the tip of his toes. He touched pieces of iron to ward away evil spirits, and everyone stepped out of his way. He came to the princess lying on the ground and he put his vibrating hands on the princess's dead body. The princess began to vibrate down to her bones. Because the vibrating man works like a machine in a modern hospital, the princess's heart began to flutter. Then it began to quiver. Then it began to beat like a drum. *Boom Boom Boom.*

The princess woke up and she hugged her father tightly and she said, "Oh, Daddy! I have learned my lesson. I am not going to marry someone who has got a nice face. I am going to marry someone who has got a good heart."

And that is the end of the story.

Commentary
Bring That Man to Me!

When reading this tale aloud you must let the energy and pace carry you along. This is a great favourite of children and I tend to tell it to large audiences in big arenas. It is the perfect assembly tale. In action it becomes a physical experience and there are a lot of opportunities for mime, acting and mimicry. There is also a call-and-response element, even when seated and reading the story. Encourage the children to anticipate and join in with the 'I KNOW A MAN' and 'BRING THAT MAN TO ME' sequences. Always allow your audience to give you energy in the telling; feed off the children's enthusiasm. Although it is you who are giving the gift, it is a shared experience where we ride the narrative together; the secret of storytelling is that you may be getting as much out of the experience as the audience.

We have a beloved princess who has her priorities wrong. Her parents should have dealt with this, but again a story begins with a death, the mother's absence, without which it could not continue. In her treatment of the other suitors she does not come across as sympathetic; indeed, this being a traditional story, she is in need of a lesson, and a lesson is what she gets.

The king is well described in the tale and we get a notion of an avuncular and easy-going man; we can relate to him. Indeed when the princess goes missing it is him we feel for, not her. He is not alone. The mysterious chamberlain, who has a seemingly inexhaustible number of old-fashioned superheroes in his Rolodex, is luckily at his side. With him the rest of the village lines up to help.

The strange characters that help with the rescue and resuscitation of the princess are a mystery. Where do they come from? How did they get this way? Whither do they go after the tale? These are questions best answered by children, for they will come up with nimble, creative and unusual answers. I recall a Chinese story with similar characters, all of them brothers. They do not go out to save others but use their abilities to get themselves out of trouble. This story is far more communal in that respect and underpins the importance of unity and togetherness. The princess has learned a lesson and the village has become stronger.

The python has a passion for princesses and this seems to be his only motivation. There are many West African tales that have animals turn into handsome men in order to get the girl, and they appear to be coming-of-age cautionary stories; in this case the snake certainly has class and knows what he's about, but it is the community that defeats him and not the wisdom of the emerging woman.

Off Road in Africa
Exercise: Off-Road Retelling

Due to the proscriptive way that we teach writing, children often see a story as a lone entity, unrelated to any other story. They see thick black lines bordering the story, containing it, and limiting it to its characters and plot. For them the story is contained within a beginning and an end, and like a 'story mountain' it lives only in two dimensions. They do not see the relationship the story has to its context and the debt it has to other stories. This reveals itself when a child finds it very difficult to change or extend an ending to a story, or to change the motivation of existing characters or introduce new ones. Children lose the sense that any story is part of a mesh of interlocking and supporting tales, some of which are merely possibilities and yet to be made.

Written stories of course are held on paper between covers, so there is a physical wall around the narrative. By contrast the oral tale changes, even minutely, every time it is told. Because it is a living, breathing entity, flexible but strong in its supporting structure, it craves change and innovation to achieve its optimum shape, and that shape changes depending on who is telling it. It is malleable in the mouth.

'I Know a Man' has reached its optimum shape for me as its teller. On other tongues, however, it can be reshaped and remodelled. This attribute makes it open to plunder and reinterpretation and it is therefore an ideal tool for children to flex their creative muscles in creating new stories from it. They become the authors of their own 'Off Road' stories. These 'potential tales' are adventures into the vista glimpsed from the path of the main story.

Ask the class the three sets of Fact, Fiction and Five Senses questions.

- Draw a 'Story Map' on the board with the help of the children. The map is a line punctuated with six or seven drawings.
- Each drawing could be a character that comes into the story from elsewhere, or an object that appears in the story.
- So the drawings for this story could be: a lake, a snake, a bird of paradise, a long nose, a thirsty tongue, a long arm, a spear, a nail. The map that you make, however, could be completely different.
- Explain to the children that a story has a life outside the map and that people and objects continue their existence when they leave the narrative.

Formulate some sample questions related to the objects you have drawn:

- What gave the snake such powers before the story began?
- What does the thirsty man do when he gets home?
- Did the man recover his spear? How did he lose it?

Ask the children, in partners, to formulate other questions.

- Make public some of their work.

- Now ask the children to make a story that answers these questions.
- The story can take place before 'I Know a Man' and lead into the main story, or it can take place when that person or thing exits the main story.

Making a story in partners is not an easy task and they may only achieve a basic storyline or set of good ideas. This is fine.

Children can note down those good ideas or even begin to create their own story map. Their story will only really begin to come to life as they tell it.

Sacred Space

This is the space at the front of the class, and the people who enter the space are worthy of respect and free from harm.

When they are ready, ask the children to enter the Sacred Space and tell their story. You will only get the bare bones of the narrative but that will be sufficient.

The importance of the Sacred Space is that it is a safe and secure environment for children to explore possibilities and to process their ideas into a coherent narrative.

Always have the audience participate with suggestions and questions to help with the processing of the story. Story making, in its first stages, is a collaborative endeavour.

If you want a writing outcome from this work please make sure that their written story is seen as a first draft. Their story is still being processed; it has not really achieved its optimum shape. Always ask the children to explain or, even better, tell the first draft of their story publicly before they produce their final piece of writing.

Quick Tips

- To get an idea of how I tackled this story check out the video story 'I Know a Man' on my website:

www.thestoryemporium.co.uk.

- Read the story through and have some gestures for 'I KNOW A MAN' (skywards-pointing finger) and 'BRING THAT MAN TO ME!' (hand flourish). Encourage the children to copy.
- Beware that there is a lot of dialogue here.
- Many story maps can generate nice works of art. It may be a good idea to devote a lesson to the drawing, reminding the children that the work may be displayed.

The Lamia

A Tale from Pakistan

The great prince Imtiaz sat astride his magnificent horse, Akbar, and he thundered down the Kashmiri valley. He was on a hunt and with him were all his courtiers; they were following him but not quite as fast. They were chasing a deer and the deer suddenly changed direction. The deer veered up the slopes of the valley and dashed into the woods. Imtiaz spurred up around and followed the deer and crashed into the woods behind it. But all his courtiers, when they rode towards the woods, their horses shied. They reared up and refused; they wouldn't go into the woods. They left Imtiaz alone, and Imtiaz followed the deer, followed the white tail of the deer. He jumped over branches, under boughs, and suddenly the deer was gone and he found himself alone in the woods. It was silent except for the bubbling and rushing of a stream.

And Imtiaz knew that Akbar was thirsty. So he trotted towards the stream. But as he got there, he saw that lying by the banks of the stream was a woman. And the woman woke up and immediately seemed frightened. She ran over to the horse, she knelt down, she held Imtiaz's foot and she said, "Sir, please have mercy! Don't hurt me! Please don't hurt me!"

Imtiaz looked down from his horse. She was a very, very beautiful woman. And he said, "I am Prince Imtiaz. I will not hurt you, lady. But tell me, who are you?"

"My name is Malia and three months ago a terrible war happened in my country and I've been trying to escape. For three months I've been sleeping in ditches and hedgerows and in woods."

She was so beautiful that Imtiaz did not notice that if she'd been sleeping rough, why was her beautiful black hair threaded with gold still in place? Why was she so clean? Why was her shalwar kameez still shining? But Imtiaz didn't think of those things because she was beautiful.

"Come, my lady. Come on the back of my horse and hang on tight." He reached down, pulled her up and she mounted the horse and put her arms around his waist. Imtiaz said, "Akbar, out of the wood! Take us home. Hyah!"

Well, when they burst out of the wood all the courtiers were there and they looked and said, "The prince is back, but look who he's got! It is definitely not a deer! She's very beautiful."

Well, Prince Imtiaz fell in love with Malia on that long ride home and took her back to his palace, his perfumed palace on the banks of the Kashmiri River. And there he decided to marry her. Well, they held a great wedding feast, but there was a problem. Every time the guests lined up to shake Imtiaz's hand, he doubled up in pain. It was as if his stomach was full of razor blades. After the wedding, the pain did not go away and so Malia said, "My dear husband, my dear prince. Send away your soothsayers, your masseurs, and your doctors. I will treat your pain by massage myself."

And she did and often the pain did go away. But at night it always returned. Imtiaz was getting sicker and sicker. And one day, he took his chamberlain and they went on a parade around the gardens. Imtiaz's gardens were bigger than some whole cities. Resting for a while, Imtiaz spotted someone in the distance lying beneath a tree. He was an old man and a poor man, dressed in rags. The chamberlain said, "Look at that cheeky toad. Let me grab him by the scruff and kick him out of your garden, sir."

"No. We are a Muslim people. If someone comes to my garden and wants to rest, they can. What you must do, chamberlain, is, without waking him, put him on a bed and surround him with food."

Well, the old man, the ragged man who was asleep, began to wake up a couple of hours later. "Oh dear, my poor back lying on the ground after all these – well, actually my back's not hurting at – woah! Look at this. I'm asleep on a bed! A gorgeous soft feather bed! This is – woah! I'm surrounded by food. Look at that! Delicious food served on gold dishes! Mmm! Tasty! Oh, that's heaven! Ohh, I'll have some of that as well! Look at all this food!"

And afterwards, he thought to himself, *I must thank the man who gave me this food. That must be the prince up there in the palace.* So the old man made his way past the Supahi into the palace. And there sat Imtiaz on his throne, pale, stroking a tiger.

The old man came up and said, "Namaste."

Imtiaz said, "As-salamu alaykum."

"Oh, thank you, thank you, my prince. You gave me a bed; you gave me food. Thank you."

Prince Imtiaz said, "What is your name, wanderer?"

"My name is Raju." The old man then looked into the eyes of the prince and saw the illness.

A good healer always looks at the eyes.

He said, "My prince, I want to pay you back. I'm a holy man and looking at you I can see that you are very ill. Do you mind if I ask you some questions? Ten only."

A good healer always asks questions.

"Yes," said the prince, "ask me your questions."

The holy man asked nine questions, and with each answer he grew more concerned. When he got to the tenth he was nervous and he said, "My dear prince, have you recently been married?"

"Yes, I have! I've married my beautiful princess, Malia."

"Uh, my prince. I think I know what's wrong with you. But to make sure, could I please cook your food for you today?"

"You can. But please remember: my princess Malia, she does not take any salt at all in her food."

"I will make sure that no salt is used," said the holy man.

He went down to the kitchens. He got a goat and killed it. Then he got the meat and rolled it in spices and cooked the meat in a tandoor. When it came to dinnertime, Imtiaz and Malia sat together. The holy man gave Imtiaz his food. But before he gave Malia her food, he secretly sprinkled three grains of salt into the meat. "I hope you enjoy your food."

Well, they did. It was excellent. Happily they went up the sandalwood stairs to bed.

But later that night, Malia woke up. "Ahh, my throat! My throat! It – It's like sandpaper! I – I must have something to drink!" She reached over for the jug of water by her bedside, but it was empty. The holy man had emptied it.

Malia was so thirsty. Holding her throat, she struggled out of the bedroom. She stumbled downstairs into the courtyard. She went to the well. She gripped the lid to lift it off the well but it would not budge. It was locked, secured by a chain. The holy man had locked it.

Now she was desperate, desperate for water. She looked at the gate; it was locked. She held the bars and peered through. She had to get to the crashing Kashmiri River outside the gate.

She had to get to the water. So she stood and looked up to the stars. Her tongue flicked out, split into two prongs and tasted the air. Her arms fused into her body, and her legs fused together; her eyes migrated to the side of her head, and her skin changed from beautiful brown to green. She had turned into a snake. And the snake slithered down towards the bars and slid through the bars, down to the Kashmiri River. And then, dislocating its jaw, it plunged its head into the river and began to drink.

Oh, the river was cool and clean and clear. And then when the snake had sated its thirst, it turned around and slithered back to the palace. But as it put its head through the bars of the gate, the holy man was waiting. He was there with an axe, a silver axe. And he raised it. It glinted in the moonlight and he brought it down on the snake's head. "Yaah!"

But the axe bounced off the scales of the neck of the snake. It spun through the air, catching the moonlight, and clattered onto the cobbled yard. And the holy man, now in panic, ran. And all the snake could hear was the retreating clacks of his sandals into the darkness. The snake slithered up the perfumed stairs and into the bedroom of Imtiaz, slithered into his bed, and then turned back into Malia the princess.

Well, the next day, the holy man came to Imtiaz and he said, "My dear Imtiaz, my dear prince. I know what's wrong with you, and the news is as bad as it can be. If a snake lives for two hundred years without being seen by a human eye, it turns into a dragon and flies to China. And if that dragon lives for a thousand years its heart grows dark and black and it turns into a lamia. A serpent! A servant of the evil one. My dear Imtiaz, my dear prince. Your wife, Malia, is a lamia! And every time she kisses you, she poisons you."

Imtiaz was taken aback. "Oh, holy man! Holy man, what am I to do?"

The holy man whispered in his ear.

So that afternoon Imtiaz summoned Malia and said, "I have spoken to the holy man and he believes I'm being poisoned by someone in the palace." The princess looked at her husband with grave concern. "Malia, he suggests that you be the only one to cook my food. Will you do that?"

"Why of course, my prince. My husband. My love. Of course I will do that."

So Prince Imtiaz built a wooden kitchen by the banks of the river and in it was a big tandoor. And he said, "Malia, come with me. Cook my food in the kitchen."

The holy man, he hid behind a bush. He looked at the kitchen. He saw two shadows going in through a gap in the wood. He saw the small shadow of Malia get some atta and begin to make rotis. He saw her then stick the rotis inside the tandoor oven. But then he saw the bigger shadow, the shadow of the prince, grab Malia and push her into the oven and close the door. All of a sudden, the whole of the kitchen caught fire.

And out of the flames came Imtiaz, his clothes smoking. Both he and the holy man watched the kitchen burn to the ground.

Many hours later, after it had cooled, both men walked around the remains of the kitchen. The holy man said, "Look, my prince. Look at that pile of white ash. That is the remains of your wife, the lamia." And then he put his hand in the white ash and brought out a jewel. A jade heart. And he said, "My dear prince, this is the heart of the lamia and this pile of white dust is the body of the lamia. Which would you like to keep?"

He said, "I will keep the heart. Thank you, holy man." And then, looking up at the Kashmiri mountains, he said, "Holy man, I regret what I have done, for I loved my wife." And he put the jewel on the remains of the tandoor oven, and then he said, "I loved her so deeply that I wonder if it was indeed better to live with her in pain, or live without her in grief. Holy man, I … Holy man …? Holy man, where are you?"

The holy man had completely vanished. But when the prince looked back at the tandoor oven, the jade heart had turned it into solid gold. And if that is what the jade heart could do, what do you think the white powder could do?

And that is the end of the story.

Commentary
Salt in the Food

For an active, rich, handsome and conscientious prince, Imtiaz is not particularly observant. He misses the clues in the forest when he first meets Malia and doesn't notice the subsequent signs regarding the poisoning. He even sends away the doctors and healers on her advice. His most obvious trait is gullibility. This is even more apparent when he accepts without question the holy man's explanation that the woman he has loved for so long is a snake.

Many traditional stories have the stain of misogyny through

them and this one shows how superstition can lead to murder. A man has to be wary when married because even that most intimate of touches, the kiss, is the gateway to death. His fear is that he has not realised that he has been sharing his bed with a snake because he has been blinded by her beauty. It is his fault for not seeing this. In this case he must beware of all women.

It has to be said that many Indian stories about the Nagin and Nagini (the male and female snake) are about true love and sacrifice, but there are still more that portray the snake as a witch or sorceress. In general, snakes, wolves and in some cases bears get a very raw deal in fairy tales, leading to some despicable pogroms against them. The prejudice against snakes is very old. In the Christian, Muslim and Jewish tradition, when Adam is in the garden it is Eve and the snake that are in another part, tearing down paradise with their diabolical curiosity. From the beginning snakes have been linked to women, and the lamia is at the apex of nastiness. The lamia has a particularly vampiric quality, and examples of its devilish work can be seen in stories from China to Greece and Spain. Some are women with the tail of a snake, others are fully female, but all have the desire to target and destroy men.

The two stand-out scenes in the tale are the journey Malia makes from the bedroom to the river and the vicious murder in the hut. The first concerns a need for water, the second the preparation of food. Both are seen through the eyes of the holy man.

The holy man, who could be seen as a charlatan, does very well out of the tale and goes away with the ability to become invisible due to the lamia's ashes. He leaves the prince feeling lost and guilty. The story does not have the triumphant ending one would expect. There is a feeling of regret and loss and it is this that perhaps redeems the tale in the end.

The Lamia in the Dock
Exercise: Hot-Seating

In children's early storytelling, and indeed in fairy tales, characters adopt a two-dimensional profile. The main interest in these cases is not psychological but in narrative; both audiences and storytellers want to know what happens next. It is when children begin to read more and read in depth that characters begin to take on value. The motivations of fictional beings begin to reflect the behaviour of the people around them and children begin to make connections and judgements. Interest in the 'inside' of a character grows as a sense of curiosity in their own make-up develops. They begin to appreciate a deeper under-standing of what makes a person.

We can begin the process of exploration of character, even for those who find reading difficult, by using the oral tale and by deeper investigation of character, using questions.

'The Lamia' is a very good story to stimulate those questions. So much seems unexplained in the story and we tend to accept without question the actions of the people involved. Without further insight we are left to assume so much about the motivation and the feelings of the people existing in the tale as the narrative cracks along. We can detect glimpses of deep feelings: betrayal, rage, despair, fear, glee, gratitude, longing and loss. We also see hints of motivation: greed, opportunism, loneliness and revenge. To be sure, however, to be certain of our guesswork, the only valid way is to get those characters in a room and ask them questions.

Ask the class the three sets of Fact, Fiction and Five Senses questions.

- Ask the children to choose a character and then pretend to be that character.

The quality of the pretence will depend on the experience that the children have of playing imaginary games. In an era of screen-based play and entertainment, that experience cannot be assumed, so praise skill in pretence and nudge others to delve deeper into wearing the mantle of the character. For most this will be such a pleasurable experience, it may even catch on in the playground.

- Remind children not to leave any characters out just because they are not main players. Akbar the horse, the chamberlain, and the many courtiers and healers in the palace deserve to have their story told.
- As a class formulate the kind of questions that will delve deep into the characters.

You will get the 'How old are you?', 'What's your favourite colour?' type of questions, and these are valid only as introductions to the person and are useful for putting the 'suspect' at ease.

- As the children divide into partners and begin their questions, encourage the children to create questions that stimulate long, detailed and thoughtful answers:
  a) 'How did you feel when ...?'
  b) 'Why did you ...?'
  c) 'What do others think about you?'
  d) 'Why do you think that ...?'

Sacred Space

This is the space at the front of the class, and the people who enter the space are worthy of respect and free from harm.

- Ask the children to step into the Sacred Space to answer questions one at a time. Provide a chair for them to sit down.

- All the children question the 'character', but be aware: if a 'character' gives an interesting answer or begins to lead the questions towards more intriguing areas, prompt incisive follow-up questions. These seek to examine thoughts, feelings and motives in more depth. They turn the questioning into more of a conversation and move the relationship between character and questioner forward, clearing the way for elaboration and clarification of details. If an adult models this, children will very swiftly catch on and copy the direction of the questions.

A writing task would be a character sketch, almost like a confession, which begins in the first person. To follow up the Oracy encourage the children to tell the story from their character's point of view.

Quick Tips

- To get an idea of how I tackled this story check out the video story 'The Lamia' on my website: www.thestoryemporium.co.uk.
- Read the story through and be aware: you may get a call out from the carpet when the lamia is first mentioned, asking for an explanation. You will find one in the commentary.
- Model some of the questions you would like to ask.
- A prop may help with getting into character on the Hot Seat. A shawl or bangle will give the speaker a boost.
- If someone is struggling, thank them and tell them to sit down with the others. Many children like to see hot-seating in action before they get it.

The Inn of the Donkeys

A Tale from China

Many centuries ago, in ancient China, there lived a merchant, and his name was Mr Chow. Now Mr Chow was a spice merchant and every year he had to make the long, arduous journey to the Perfumed City to sell his spices; and it came to that time of year, so he readied his donkey whose name was Ling. "Come on, Ling."

And he got on top of Ling, put the spices behind him, and they began the journey.

Well, it was a long, long journey and it was a very hot day and poor old Mr Chow with the sun beating down on his shoulders and on his head, and the rhythm of the swaying donkey, and the beat of the donkey's hooves on the road – *clip, clop, clip, clop* – his eyelids felt heavy, and he fell fast asleep.

Now, it's all right to fall asleep on a donkey, because the donkey will take you where you want to go, as long as it knows the route. Ling was a very intelligent donkey. However, as the way wound up through the mountains, Ling saw that a tree had fallen down and blocked the entire path, just in front of him. And Ling said, "Oh dear, oh dear, there is a tree blocking the path, and I don't know what I should do. I cannot climb over the tree, because Mr Chow is asleep on my back, and I do not want to wake him up. So I suppose I'll take another route. I think I'll go … this way."

Ling turned, went off the path, and went into the forest. It was a very deep, thick forest, but there was an animal trail through the trees, and Ling followed the animal trail. After about five hours, Ling and Mr Chow emerged from the forest into a beautiful valley that was cut through by a snow-fed, fast-flowing, icy, crystal-clear mountain stream.

Well, by now Mr Chow began to wake up. "Oh dear, oh, I must have fallen asleep. Sorry, Ling, I'm sorry I'm always doing – whoa! Look at that mountain! I don't recognise it at all! Wow! Ling, where have you brought me? We're not on the path."

Well, luckily for him there was a man, standing up to his knees in the river. He was a peasant. Mr Chow, well, he stopped Ling and said, "Hello there! Good morning."

"Good morning."

"I'm sorry to disturb you but I'm very lost. Um, do you know where we are?"

"Yes. Yes I do." But the man said nothing further.

"My dear man, I'm very tired and I'd love a place to stay. Is there a hotel around here or some kind of an inn?"

"Oh yes, there is. There is an inn about a mile up there, over the wooden bridge; there you will find the Inn of the Donkeys. A very beautiful lady called Third Lady owns the Inn of the Donkeys and she always has room. So please, go for a mile, cross the wooden bridge, to the Inn of the Donkeys."

"Thank you very much, peasant. Have a good day."

So Mr Chow and Ling crossed the wooden bridge and went up to the Inn of the Donkeys. There it was by the side of the stream. It looked quite beautiful; it was a large wooden house, two storeys, with a roof that bent up at the ends, and with a high brick wall surrounding it.

Ling took Mr Chow in through the courtyard, and there, coming out of the door, was a very beautiful woman with high cheekbones, full lips and a charming smile whose hair was as black as the bottom of a well. So this must be Third Lady. She bowed.

"You are very welcome to my inn, merchant. Please, would you mind stabling your own donkey? I'm afraid I do not have any servants. Then come and join me for something to eat."

"Of course. It will be my pleasure," said Mr Chow. "Come along, Ling." And he led Ling to the stable.

But when they got to the stable it was full of donkeys tied tightly to metal rings in the brick walls. But those donkeys looked strange: they quivered and they trembled. They made no sound; their lips stretched back, showing their big teeth. Their eyes were as big as saucers. Ling's eyes stretched, because those donkeys weren't just afraid; they were terrified.

Mr Chow said to Ling, "Now, Ling, listen. Don't look at those donkeys. I don't want you getting upset, okay? Now you stay here and eat your food, because, my dear friend, I'm going inside to eat my food. I'm starving."

Mr Chow entered the inn to find about twenty other merchants in the Common Room sitting in groups and chatting. Mr Chow joined them and warmed his hands by the fire; it was getting to be quite a cool night.

The merchants were talking about the goods they had to sell, and each of them held a cup, and through them gracefully glided Third Lady, filling up the merchants' cups with Ngo wine, and Ngo wine is a very, very strong rice wine. She filled up Mr Chow's cup and smiled at him.

"Oh, thank you very much." But Mr Chow, he didn't really like alcohol, so when no one was looking, he poured his Ngo wine into a flowerpot. "Oh, it's very good, isn't it?" he fibbed. "An excellent example of good wine, isn't it?"

"Gentlemen," said Third Lady, "would you please put out the boards?"

"Well, of course we will," said the merchants, and they set out the tables and sat down. Third Lady brought each of them a steaming bowl of beautiful perfumed jasmine rice. Some of it was covered with crackly honeyed pork and some of it was covered with monk's vegetables, and all of the merchants ate very well.

Third Lady then came in, collected the dishes and said, "My guests, would you please mind putting away the boards? It is time to sleep."

"Yes, Third Lady. Goodnight, Third Lady," replied the merchants.

They put away the boards and they unrolled their mattresses and their sheets and all of them got in, and within seconds they were all asleep; because Ngo wine makes you very, very sleepy. But Mr Chow, he couldn't sleep, because Ngo wine also makes you snore, and the sound coming out of the merchants was like a dragon roaring in a drain! The whole house shook like a ship in a storm, and poor Mr Chow, he couldn't get to sleep. But there was another sound, beneath the rumbling, the sound of something heavy being moved.

Mr Chow was curious. He got up, and he made his way down the corridor; he made his way to where the sound was coming from – Third Lady's bedroom. In the screen of wood, there was a little crack, and he looked through and saw Third Lady dragging a big, heavy, brown, carved box out from under a blanket. She then brought out a key hung around her neck; she opened the box, put her hand inside, and pulled out a package, an oilskin package.

Mr Chow watched, unmoving. She unwrapped the package and took out a wooden figure of a man, and she put that wooden figure on the floorboards. The man just stared at her. Then she took out the wooden figure of an ox; she put that down as well. And then, lastly, a small plough. She put it down, and then she took a cup with some water, put the water in her mouth, went over to the figures on the floor and sprayed them with her water. And as soon as the water touched the wooden man, he came alive. He looked at Third Lady, and he saluted, and then he hitched the ox to the plough; he then began ploughing up the floorboards, and the floorboards lifted and splintered. He stopped when he had made eight long furrows with his plough.

The little wooden man then put his hand into his wooden coat and pulled out a bag, a bag of seeds; he opened it and broadcast the seeds all over the ploughed wooden floor. Pausing, he also drank some water and sprayed the seeds. Immediately, the seeds began to grow, higher, and higher, until within a minute they were a foot tall: green stalks of wheat, and as the little wooden man unhitched the oxen, the green wheat turned golden yellow. The little wooden man wiped his forehead and took out a sickle for cutting wheat and he walked beside the furrows cutting the wheat, and when he'd stopped he put the sickle inside his belt, looked at Third Lady, saluted her, and froze again, as a wooden man.

Third Lady put the figures back into the oilskin, wrapped it up and put it back in the box. She took the stalks of wheat, shook them out and blew away the chaff. She then crushed the ears until she'd made flour. And with the flour, she spat on it, and she began to make cakes, little cakes. She made twenty-one little cakes, baked them in the oven, and the smell of the cakes permeated the whole of the room.

Mr Chow was amazed at what he'd seen; this was magic! He was also frightened. He had best keep his mouth shut because Third Lady was surely a witch. He made his way back to the Common Room and got inside his blanket, but he did not sleep that night.

The next morning the merchants woke up in a cheery mood. "Ah, lovely, that was such a good sleep. Right, better get the donkeys ready." And they all went outside to the courtyard to load up their donkeys.

In the courtyard was Third Lady, and she was carrying a tray of cakes, the same cakes she'd made last night. She announced to them all, "My dear guests, it would be remiss of me to send you on your way without giving you any breakfast. Please, have one of my cakes." She made sure she gave every single merchant a cake.

Mr Chow took the cake, but instead of eating it he put it in his sleeve. The rest of the merchants, they munched away merrily. "Mmm, Third Lady, that was absolutely lovely. Best breakfast this side of the Perfumed City."

Mr Chow quickly unhitched Ling and said, "I can't tell you anything now, Ling, but come with me quick. We've got to get out of here!" They slipped out of the courtyard and got about a hundred yards away, but Mr Chow was curious. What was going to happen? He tied Ling up and said, "Ling, stay there. Look, don't sulk, I'll tell you later. Just stay there. I've got to go and see what's happening."

He ran to the wall, scrambled up an apple tree and looked over. The merchants were still milling around the courtyard; one merchant was talking loudly. "Yes, I've got some bright copper wire and I'm taking it to the town of Singing Kettles. Yeah, ha ha ha, the prices they pay there, they're absolutely *heeeux*trordinary. Oops, sorry about that, ha ha, I sounded just like a donkey, didn't I? I sound*heeeh haw*, oh, *hee haw*, oh, *hee haw*, oh, *hee haw*, *hee haw*, *hee haw*."

All the other merchants began to laugh, and as they laughed, they too made donkey sounds. "Ha, ha, ha, ha, did you hear him? Ha ha, *hee haw*, oh."

Then suddenly the pain began. Thick, stiff hairs began to emerge and push their way through each of the merchants' skins, on his face, on his neck, on his arms! All of a sudden all the merchants' skulls split, and their eyes were pushed to the sides of their heads as their jaws elongated and grew forward. One of the merchants, he wanted to run; he turned, he ran towards the entrance to the courtyard, but his tail pushed through his trousers and caught on a nail. Their arms stiffened and their hips cracked as their legs twisted so their knees faced backwards. All of them fell to the floor as their spines broke, and their hands and feet petrified into hooves, and they screamed in pain and agony.

When they'd finished changing into donkeys, Third Lady emerged once again and she said, "Merchants, you are no longer human. You are donkeys now, my donkeys. And I mean to sell you, which is why I gave you the cakes. But, before I sell you, you must learn to obey." She unfurled a huge leather whip and began laying about her mercilessly.

Mr Chow, so frightened now, he turned, he ran to Ling and when he unhooked Ling, Ling looked at him. "What's going on here?"

But Mr Chow didn't tell him, because Ling heard the screams of the donkeys being whipped and somehow he knew. "Quick, Ling, quick! Quick! Let's get to the Perfumed City!"

By the end of the day, they'd reached the Perfumed City, and Mr Chow had sold all his spices. But still he was worried. He couldn't tell anyone what he'd seen; they would accuse him of being an enchanter and spreading terrible rumours. He was also ashamed that he didn't help the unfortunate merchants. So he went upstairs to the teahouse where he would spend the night and he took off his robe, and out of his robe dropped the cake that Third Lady had given him. He remembered stashing it up his sleeve. He picked up the cake and he said, "What kind of magic is in this cake? This is just like the cake they sell on the streets down there – it's just like the cakes they sell on the streets!" He opened up his window; he shouted out, "Hey you, boy!"

"Yeah, what do you want?"

"Those cakes you're selling – bring six of them up to me."

"I'll be right up!"

The boy came up with six of the cakes and Mr Chow gave him the money. Mr Chow got the cakes, he put them in a handkerchief, but he put Third Lady's cake on top. Now he had seven cakes.

The next morning he got Ling. "Ling, we're going back to the Inn of the Donkeys."

"Hee haw, hee haw, hee haw, hee haw!"

"Now, now, don't fuss. Trust me, Ling, trust me. I mean to right an injustice."

So Ling and Mr Chow made their way back to the Inn of the

Donkeys. They walked into the courtyard, and Third Lady was there.

"Good morning, merchant, it is good to see you. Would you please stable your own donkey, for I have no servants, and then come and join me for something to eat."

Great! thought Mr Chow. *She doesn't recognise me.* He stabled the donkey and went in.

The same as before, the food was excellent – the jasmine rice, the pork; he didn't drink the Ngo wine. As before, he got up in the middle of the night, peered through the screen and saw her with the little wooden man, ploughing the floorboards, and saw her making the cakes.

The next morning, when he'd saddled Ling, Third Lady came out.

"Merchant, it would be remiss of me to send you away without some breakfast. Please, have one of my cakes."

"Oh!" said Mr Chow. "I'd be delighted! Yes, I definitely will have one of your cakes; but you've been such a great hostess, why don't I give you one of mine first? I bought these in the Perfumed City." He offered the cakes to Third Lady.

Third Lady said, "I never eat cakes. I'm always baking them but I never eat them. From the Perfumed City, you say? Well then, yes, of course I'll have one of your cakes, but you must have one of mine."

"Of course," said Mr Chow. "But you first. Try that one. What does it taste like?"

"Well, it's delicious, merchant, absolutely – *hee haw!*" She realised! "You've tricked me! You've tricked me! You've tri*hee haw! Hee haw! Hee haw!*"

She began to change and she was in agony as her whole body transformed into a donkey. But still her eyes glared at Mr Chow, and they were eyes of anger, rage and hate.

Mr Chow looked at the donkey. "Well, Third Lady, now you've got a taste of your own medicine. Ling! Now you've got someone to share a stable with."

Ling glowered at his new stable mate.

Well, Ling and Mr Chow took Third Lady as a donkey back to the town where he lived. He used Third Lady like a heavy horse. Whenever there was a huge mountain to climb and the load was really heavy, Third Lady did it. Whenever he had to cross a river and the river came up to his eyebrows, Third Lady did that job. Third Lady did all the heavy jobs for Mr Chow. After the first year, Third Lady was still energetic, but after the fifth year, Third Lady now, when she walked, she stumbled along.

Mr Chow was riding Third Lady through the city, when he saw a merchant friend of his who'd been out of the country for a long while, but he had such a battered-up face he must have had a hard time.

"Hello there, Mr Ho!"

"Mr Chow, it's good to see you! Haven't seen you in a long time. I've had a terrible adventure, and – just a minute, Mr Chow, your donkey ... I know this donkey!"

He went round to the head of the donkey and said, "I know you, Third Lady! Mr Chow, this Third Lady turned me into a donkey and I worked down the mines for a whole year, and my master was so cruel and he beat me often. I always think about you, Third Lady. How long have you had her, Mr Chow?"

"Well, she's been doing a lot of work for me. I've had her five years."

"Five years? Five years as a donkey is a long time. I'm beginning to feel sorry for Third Lady."

"Well, so am I," said Mr Chow. "But I don't know how to turn her back."

"That's easy," said Mr Ho.

He took out a muleteer's skinner's knife and he went to the donkey and said, "Third Lady, just be calm now, be calm now." He laid the blade of the knife next to Third Lady's stomach. "Be calm." He suddenly twisted the blade and cut Third Lady's stomach open! Immediately, Third Lady fell out of the donkey, and the donkey's skin and bones collapsed and crumbled all around her.

Third Lady got up and looked at Mr Ho.

"Mr Ho, thank you for releasing me. I apologise for the pain that I have caused you. And you, Mr Chow, I won't forget you!" With that she turned and disappeared into the crowd, making her way into another story.

And that is the end of the story.

Commentary
Third Lady

Transforming into a donkey usually seems to be either a punishment, as in the story of Pinocchio, or as an unintended consequence of messing about with magic as happens to Lucius in Apuleius' 'The Golden Ass'. Here it seems to be for profit, pure and simple. It also seems to have been going on for rather a long time. Third Lady has been at it for at least six years, but one suspects by the efficiency of her methods, perhaps a lot longer. At the end of the tale Mr Ho claims he worked in the mines for a year, so there is an endpoint to the spell. Once Third Lady has made her money from the sale, she doesn't seem to be interested in any form of product guarantee. I detect a prejudice against the single businesswoman in this Chinese story, but she remains a powerful figure, cool and aloof, and being alone in the company of men, very self-assured.

There is a hierarchy of control in the story. Mr Chow controls Ling, Third Lady controls the merchants, and at the bottom is the strange figure of the wooden man. Although this is foul magic the wooden figures are intriguing. We are compelled to ask who they are, how they got into this state and what their future is, after the story finishes. I can find no other spells and enchantments quite like this in other tales. I believe this archetype is probably the genesis of the story and the Mr Chow point of view a later addition.

The shock in the story comes with the transformation of the merchants. The panic and pain is horrific and we realise that the donkeys in the stable ('Their eyes were as big as saucers') were also merchants and that this is a production line.

Indeed this business has been very well thought out. The Ngo wine is soporific and the cakes she produces are poison, so Third Lady breaks all the rules of hospitality, let alone enslaving her guests by means of the wooden figures. The cold way that she witnesses the transformations of the merchants and her use of the whip gives her a powerful detachment. Without doubt she is a witch, and an audience would enjoy her comeuppance; her punishment is certainly cruel.

The power of stories like this is proved by the persecution of women as witches – often old, often poor and alone – up to modern times. It is an aspect of fairy tales that sits uneasily with a modern storyteller. I am glad that she is redeemed and that she is free at the end. I feel sure that she will thrive and be successful, but as what?

Inn of the Donkeys
Exercise: Changing the Setting

Settings are so often disregarded in children's writing, and as such they reflect the value placed on them by oral yarns, fairy tales and traditional stories. A wood is a wood, a mountain, a mountain. A palace, a village, a city, a desert – these are all merely backdrops or colour schemes in front of which the narrative takes place. In fairy tales and traditional stories, though, setting also functions as a transportation device to place the listener in the actual world of the tale or give notice that the story is of the past and from a place that does not necessarily exist. Much of children's early writing focuses exclusively on the movement of the narrative and could successfully ignore setting altogether.

This is the challenge we face when seeking to guide children to enrich their writing. Setting is fundamental to a well-crafted written story. It should infect and influence character and plot and be so much part of the fabric of the story that it becomes an indissoluble part of the solution. This can be hard to explain if we tack setting on to a tale as an afterthought; it should be there from the beginning. A way to help children to appreciate the function of setting is to take it away from a story or change it, and then see how the story itself changes.

'The Inn of the Donkeys' is set in China, although it is a China that could exist at any time during the two thousand years before the twentieth century. It is a told story, so the setting has the minor function of placing the tale away from the here and the now. This makes the tale a good model for changing the setting and seeing how that affects the narrative and the characters.

Ask the class the three sets of Fact, Fiction and Five Senses questions.

- Ask the children to list a number of settings, both geographical and temporal.
- Ideas will range from modern housing estates to classrooms in a US high school, but also prompt them by allowing bizarre and unusual suggestions, for example Victorian times, under the sea, in the world of insects, on the moon or as Greek gods.
- In partners ask the children to retell the story of 'The Inn of the Donkeys' using a different setting.
- Tell them that they will notice that many things have to change: Ling has to become a car or spaceship or steam train; the cakes have to become biscuits or alien fruit or candy.
- Remind them to also notice that characters' motivations

change: Mr Chow might be on his way to Jupiter for a wedding; Third Lady might be changing small boys into chimney sweeps.

- Ask them to think about clothing, food, transport and what the new inn will look like.

Sacred Space

This is the space at the front of the class, and the people who enter the space are worthy of respect and free from harm.

- As always, when you believe the children are finished ask them to come into the Sacred Space to tell their stories.

Quick Tips

- To get an idea of how I tackled this story check out the video story 'The Inn of the Donkeys' on my website: www.thestoryemporium.co.uk.
- Read the story through. If you need to split the telling into two sessions, stop when Mr Chow flees to the Perfumed City. In the second session ask the children to remind you what happened before you continue.
- Choose some pictures for different settings and display them to the children: Dubai at night, a rainforest, a coral reef etc.
- Ask the children to remember the Five Senses question and apply it to their new setting.
- Drawing the setting may be useful for the children.

Spirit Foxes

A Tale from Japan

Well, a long, long, long time ago in ancient Japan, and right at the top of Japan, in a place called Sapporo, there was a village and it was always cold in the village. The villagers kept themselves warm by telling warm stories.

One day a baby was born in the village, a baby boy, a very, very big baby boy. His name was Ryuichi and the big baby boy Ryuichi grew up to be a big bully. He pushed everybody around in the village.

Sometimes he would just come up to a hut, kick the door down, walk in when the family was sitting around eating, then he would push the daddy out of his chair, then he would sit in the daddy's chair and eat the daddy's food and after that he would steal the children's food. The people couldn't do anything about him, this bully, because there were no police around. But what scandalised and hurt them the most, what they could not bear was that Ryuichi would make fun of their beliefs.

Everybody in the village believed in the spirit foxes. All around the village and all around the neighbourhood, silver foxes would run at night. The villagers believed that these were spirit foxes; these silver foxes had the spirits of the ancestors inside them.

So one day, all the villagers marched along through the streets of the village, up to Ryuichi's hut and banged on the door.

Ryuichi came to the door. "Yeah! Yeah! What do you want? This better be good."

The villagers cowered back from the door, because even in a crowd they were scared of Ryuichi. The headman said, "Ryuichi, we are fed up of you disrespecting our beliefs."

Ryuichi burst out laughing. "You stupid mongrels, there are

no such things as spirit foxes! Of course I disrespect your stupid beliefs. It's all a load of rubbish and you are all idiots for believing it."

"Well," said the headman, "you wouldn't say that if you spent one night in the meadow and then maybe you would be convinced."

"Ha ha ha! One night in the meadow? Yeah! All right then, all right then, I'll do it. But listen to me: if I don't see any spirit foxes, I'm going to come back here and each one of you is going to give me money. Ha ha ha ha! Idiots."

Well, that night Ryuichi made his way up to the meadow. He brought his roll-up blanket, put it on the ground and lay on it, looking at the stars. It was a cold night, and he pulled his blanket up tight, but it was not a silent night, for when the darkness fell Ryuichi could hear all the animals wake up, come to life and move around in the night time.

He could hear rustling through the grass, barks and howls from the forest, and although Ryuichi would never tell anybody else, he was very frightened. But he did manage to get a little sleep.

In the morning he woke up. "Ah! Well, I've done it! I've spent a night in the meadow, and I haven't seen any stupid spirit foxes!!" He looked up on the ridge and his smile froze. Because there, silhouetted against the rising sun, was a fox, a silver fox.

Ryuichi looked at it. It looked back at him. The silver fox then turned and started to trot along the ridgeline. Ryuichi said, "That's nothing special; it's just a dirty scavenger. I'm going to follow that fox. Yeah. Every step of the way. I'm going to prove to them that there are no such things as spirit foxes. I'm going to see what it does."

So he left his rolled blanket on the ground, and sped after the fox. He followed the fox for a few miles, but the fox never turned round. Then the fox went into a grove of oak and silver birch trees, and Ryuichi thought, *I might lose him; I might lose him in the woods. I'll run round the other side so I can wait for him to come out.*

As fast as anything, he ran round the grove and waited for the fox. But the fox did not come out; instead, what came out of the grove was a young girl. A girl around Ryuichi's age; Ryuichi watched her. Then he saw that the girl's jet-black hair had a streak of silver in it.

"Ooh! It's true! It's true, she's a fox, and she's a spirit fox. She's turned back into her human form. I'm going to follow her. I'm going to follow her and I'm going to capture her, and take her back to the village. I'm going to show those idiots that I'm not scared of no spirit fox."

So he followed the girl through the trees, and the girl went into a clearing. And in the clearing there was a hut. Ryuichi crouched low and watched her go into the hut. He stood up and walked across the clearing and he looked down. "I'm right, it *is* a spirit fox. I'm right. Look, chicken bones, bird bones, rabbit bones. All scattered around the hut. This is where it eats its prey. This is the clearing of one of them spirit foxes, all right. Well, I'm going to catch that girl."

He went up to the door of the hut, and he kicked it down quite easily – remember, he was very used to kicking down doors – and he strode into the darkness.

In the dark hut were an old man, an old lady and the girl. And the old man said, "Hey, hey! Who are you? What do you want?"

"Be quiet, old man. That girl, she is a spirit fox, and I'm going to take her down to the village. Tied up if I have to!"

The family stood up and looked very cautiously at the intruder. "I am not a fox, I'm a girl! Are you out of your mind?" said the girl. "You stay away from me!"

Ryuichi tried to grab her but she struggled. She pulled away from him and ran for the door. He caught her by the hair. She kicked him hard. So he picked her up and threw her against the wall, but there was a metal spike on the wall and she banged her head on the spike and she fell down. Ryuichi stepped back.

The old woman screamed, "What have you done? What have you done?" She knelt down by the girl, she saw the blood coming out, and she said, "You've killed her, you've killed my daughter! You've killed her."

Ryuichi said, "No, no, she's no girl; she's a fox."

"She's not a fox, you stupid man. You've killed my daughter. Can't you see her lying there? She's my daughter!" The old man spoke quietly. "You broke into our house. You murdered my daughter. You took her away from us. For that you must pay."

Then he jumped on Ryuichi and grabbed him by the arms, and a struggle took place. The old man was stronger than he looked. Well, the old lady, she got up and she got a shovel and she swung it at Ryuichi's shins, with the blade end. He collapsed.

The old man sat on him and tied his hands behind his back; the old woman tied his ankles together, and then pulled him over. Then the old man said, "You nasty, nasty man, you murdered my daughter and we're going to kill you for it. It is what you deserve."

Just then, the door opened, and in walked a holy man. "Peace to all here. Ooh! What is going on? Why have you tied up this young man?"

The old man said, "Oh, holy man, oh, Your Eminence, this man, he came into our hut, and he's just killed our daughter. He's murdered our daughter."

"Oh dear, oh dear," said the holy man and he knelt by the lifeless body of the girl. "And what do you propose to do with this criminal?"

"We are going to kill him," said the old woman quietly.

The holy man stood up and sighed. "No, don't do that, because if you do that, you'll be just like him. I understand the pain you must be feeling. I have a suggestion, if the criminal agrees; I shall take him as one of my followers to spend his life with me, learning my ways, doing good works. In time he may come to realise the harm he has done. What do you think?"

Ryuichi looked at the holy man and thought, *Oh yeah, I could get away with this. Yeah, I'll just follow the man for a couple of months. Pretend to be all sorry and stuff. I could get away with murder, yeah, small price to pay.* He set his face to sorrowful and pleaded with the holy man, "Yes, yes, I'd like to be your follower, master."

The old man said, "But, holy man, he murdered my daughter."

"Do not worry, old man. Being my follower is very hard. The first thing you have to do, young man, is to shave your head. Do you have a razor?"

Ryuichi said, "No, master, I don't."

The old man said, "I do, a really rusty blunt one."

So the old man and the old woman spent a long hour shaving Ryuichi's head with their rusty blade. His eyes watered and he screamed loudly. When they had finished he was exhausted.

"Now you must be tattooed on the head with my symbol," said the holy man. "This is the symbol of truth."

"Let me do that," demanded the old woman. "I have the needles!"

So the old man, the old woman and the holy man tattooed Ryuichi all over his head with the symbol. It was very very painful but Ryuichi thought, *Well, I can put up with this because I am getting away with murder.*

It took most of the day, but when they were finished they stepped back and examined their work. Then the holy man said, "Now you will be my follower. You will go where I go. That is, if you can find me …" *Poof!* And the holy man disappeared!

Ryuichi said, "Did you see that? Did you see that? Where did he go? He just vanished!"

He turned to the old man, and the old man waved his hand and said, "Bye bye." *Psshh!* He disappeared.

The old woman said, "Aah, it's over." *Psshh!* And she disappeared.

Ryuichi looked around; he was on his own in the hut, alone,

except for the dead girl.

He looked at her. He knelt beside her and for the first time he felt very sorry for what he had done. But then she sat up. She winked at him, grinned, and she disappeared. Then the hut disappeared, then the clearing disappeared. Ryuichi sat in the middle of the woods. "What's going on? This is driving me crazy! What's going on?"

Then when he looked up he saw the ridge. Silhouetted against the setting sun he saw four silver spirit foxes look down at him, wag their tails, and then run into the growth of the trees. Ryuichi was terrified, and he ran and ran and did not stop until he got to the middle of the village. There he halted and called everyone together, shouting, "It's true, it's true, it's true, I tell you! The spirit foxes! They're real! Come listen to my story."

But all the villagers looked at him. They just pointed and they laughed; they laughed and laughed and clutched their sides. Because tattooed all over Ryuichi's shaved head was 'I am an idiot'. And in the olden days, you couldn't get rid of tattoos.

And that is the end of the story.

Commentary
Idiot for Life

The set-up to the story is a portrayal of powerlessness. The enemy comes from within, a child from the village. The child has grown up and breaks the boundaries of convention in that society. The villagers cannot stop him by physical force; he is too strong. He cannot be made accountable; there is no justice system. They have failed in their guidance of the child and now they are suffering the thuggery of the man.

Ryuichi is iconoclastic and anarchic in equal measure. It isn't clear what he really wants and he just seems happy to feel the joy of dominating others. In this way he resembles the archetypal school bully, a brute. In this case, though, there is no higher authority to curb his behaviour; even parents and elders suffer from his persecution.

The main source of their anguish is the contempt he has for their beliefs. In many ways this is 'story' asserting itself. Ryuichi laughs at the idea that local foxes contain the spirits of the dead, but then most traditional stories contain the ridiculous, be it a wolf jumping into bed wearing Granny's nightie, or a beanstalk with a giant at the top. This story sets out to prove 'story's assertion' that anything is possible and nothing is certain. We may support Ryuichi's scepticism, if not his discourtesy, but to enjoy the story we have to leave science and empiricism at the door and engage with fantasy in order to reveal different truths about being human.

The challenge is taken and Ryuichi sets out into the countryside. He is genuinely disconcerted to see the fox turn into a girl, but he nimbly forgets his disbelief. He shifts the emphasis away from proving the spirit foxes as false, to proving that he does not fear them. He is an opportunist rather than a sceptic, further diminishing him, and setting him up for a well-deserved fall. To further his retribution the foxes are revealed to be a young girl and an older couple, all very vulnerable when compared with Ryuichi's might.

The struggle in the hut and the girl's murder are shocking and bring the listener up sharp; up until now this has been a fairly amusing tale with intriguing revelations, but the metal spike, the lifeless body and the old ones' grief suddenly make the story stark and abrupt. There is a genuine fear that the old people will take their revenge, which would diminish them both, and so it is some relief when the holy man enters.

The shaving with the rusty blade and the painful tattoo procedure go some way towards retribution, but Ryuichi laughing at them, knowing he will get away with murder, offsets this. Japanese stories are renowned for their misdirection and in this case we are taken in; the wearing of masks in Noh theatre and in the Japanese military makes the point that what seems is rarely what is. It should come as a surprise to all when the humans disappear; particularly astonishing and wry is the girl's wink and grin as she disappears. Ryuichi's dash to the village is the final act in his humiliation. It is apt that at the end he wears a constant reminder of this, a reminder, like belief in the spirit foxes, that everyone else can see but he can't. A good lesson that an effective way to oppose tyranny is to laugh at it.

Calm Down and Tell Me What Happened
Exercise: Point-of-View Retelling

Much of the story of 'Spirit Foxes' happens outside the narrative. Do the foxes contrive to trick Ryuichi from the very beginning or do they improvise a response when they encounter him entering the clearing? Have the villagers conspired with the foxes the whole time or is the appearance of the bully with his ridiculous tattoo a genuine surprise?

This is the inevitable consequence of having the story told in the third person.

The story is told in the third person so that the storyteller can control events and deal with multi-character scenes. It is an intriguing conceit. It means that there is always another person in the setting with the characters. It is the audience in the form of the storyteller who is in the meadow with Ryuichi when he first spots the fox, and there are more than five people in the small hut in the clearing: Ryuichi, the old man, the old woman, the young girl, the holy man, and of course us, the audience, in the form of the storyteller, sitting and watching events unfold.

The problem of having the third person relate the story is that the narrator cannot see what is not in front of him or her. We cannot have the questions about what happens outside the narrative answered. We need to ask someone who is there. We need to have the tale told again, this time from a specific character's point of view.

Telling a story from a specific character's point of view means telling in the first person and this does not initially come easily to children, despite the fact of it being the norm in video games. Children have to be reminded constantly to use the pronoun 'I' and to be aware not to relate events they could not possibly have seen as that character. Eventually they will settle into that particular seat and drive the narrative forward. They will find a refreshing surge of energy when telling, because for them it feels like a completely different story to which they know all the words. It can be the breakthrough for reluctant storytellers.

The audience watching a first-person retelling also feels slightly different. They are not in the story. There are only five people in the hut now, and only one sees the fox in the meadow.

Ask the class the three sets of Fact, Fiction and Five Senses questions.

- Ask the children to choose a character each, then in their partner groups retell the story from their point of view.
- One partner is the teller and one the checker. The checker has to constantly remind the teller to use 'I' and should be armed with the statement, 'You couldn't know that; you weren't there.'
- A useful launch-off point would be to suggest that the story is over and your character has run home to his mum. The mum greets the character and asks, 'What happened to you?' The story will then flow from there.
- The teller also has to keep in mind the times when they are not in the story. They do not cease to exist; they are somewhere else while the story continues, so remind them that they have to make those bits up.
- The improvised scenes need to be nimble and appropriate to the story.
- After a time, swap over and continue.

Sacred Space

This is the space at the front of the class, and the people who enter the space are worthy of respect and free from harm.

- Have the children enter the Sacred Space and publicly tell.

If all goes well and you have identified some nimble tellers, set them the far harder challenge to continue to tell the story from the first-person point of view but in the present tense. They will discover an immediacy and vitality to their telling that will excite their audience but also amaze themselves.

Quick Tips

- To get an idea of how I tackled this story check out the video story 'Spirit Foxes' on my website: www.thestoryemporium.co.uk.
- Practise the story and try a particular 'look' for Ryuichi. He drives most of the tale and it would be useful to practise a sneering face.
- Slow right down for the last two lines.
- Whoever the children choose for their first-person retell, ask them to do the walk or the face of the character.
- Filming some of the retellings would be very useful to reinforce the first-person narrative and a good stimulus for diary or letter writing.

And That Is the Start of the Story

Review

A quick checklist of the impact storytelling will have on your practice:

- An understanding and appreciation of why storytelling and Oracy are fundamental to learning
- A keener understanding and awareness of children's voice
- An understanding of how to use the drama and Oracy exercises associated with the storytelling
- A more secure classroom management practice while encouraging children's Oracy
- A greater confidence when ceding the vocal space to children
- A more refreshed and revitalized practice when linking elements of storytelling to all other aspects of the curriculum using key questions and mapping.

Throughout this book I have urged you 'To Think', 'To Do' and 'To See':

- To think – about the nature and power of stories
- To do – the telling of stories
- To see – your observations of children.

When you *think*, I hope by my stance and approach that you will consider changing the paradigm that we find ourselves operating in. I hope you will see that the learning involved in storytelling, together with speaking and listening, is not a linear process to be measured in terms of time and motion; it is organic and takes place at different rates. It depends on setting up an environment that is safe and secure but also vivid and exciting. Telling a story cannot be successful if it is meticulously planned and fretted over. It needs a relaxed and easy approach. It needs an equality of status, a trust and bond between teller and audience, a true sharing. The least of the outcomes is collective joy and that is a jumping-off point for all other learning endeavours.

When you *do*, by reading these tales aloud to children, I hope that you will begin to discover the glory of the experience. One of the greatest gifts we can give to children is to discover the artist in ourselves. An artistic act is a generous one. It does not require equal exchange, but it does ask for a response. It is the artistic act itself and the authentic and heartfelt response of children that constitute deep developmental learning. When you read a story to children, and then armed with that skill and experience, tell it to them, you begin to develop yourself as an artist. It is essential that your discovery of the joy and growth that telling a story brings is revealed to the children who, great imitators that they are, will recognise the pleasure and seek the adventure. I hope that you decide to make storytelling a language habit in your class. I hope that you discover the artist in yourself and recognise the artist in them.

When you *see*, I hope you see the children. You will see the short termism of forcing conformity on such diversity. All children are unique; there has never been another one like them, and they will display their infinite diversity when they speak. They will reveal themselves through the exercises, they will learn to use their language in the Sacred Space, and they will experience a notion that leads to a thought, which forms a word, which makes a sound. They will begin to think.

If we could predict the future we could train them for it. We can't. The best way to prepare them to embrace whatever future they encounter is to arm them with a free and valued imagination and the means to express themselves confidently and with power. The best way is to tell them stories.

Liberalis is a Latin word which evokes ideas of freedom, liberality, generosity of spirit, dignity, honour, books, the liberal arts education tradition and the work of the Greek grammarian and storyteller Antonius Liberalis. We seek to combine all these interlinked aspects in the books we publish.

We bring classical ways of thinking and learning in touch with traditional storytelling and the latest thinking in terms of educational research and pedagogy in an approach that combines the best of the old with the best of the new.

As classical education publishers, our books are designed to appeal to readers across the globe who are interested in expanding their minds in the quest of knowledge. We cater for primary, secondary and higher education markets, homeschoolers, parents and members of the general public who have a love of ongoing learning.

If you have a proposal that you think would be of interest to Liberalis, submit your inquiry in the first instance via the website: www.liberalisbooks.com.